Walks For All Ages
Peak District

WALKS FOR ALL AGES

PEAK DISTRICT

NORMAN TAYLOR

Published by Bradwell Books
11 Orgreave Close Sheffield S13 9NP
Email: books@bradwellbooks.co.uk

British Library Cataloguing in Publication Data: a catalogue record for this book is available from the British Library.

1st Edition

ISBN: 9781909914018

Printed and bound by CPI Group (UK) Ltd, Croydon, CR0 4YY

Design by: Erik Siewko Creative, Derbyshire.
eriksiewko@gmail.com

Photograph Credits: © Norman Taylor
Except Page 72 © National trust images / Joe Cornish
and Page 73 © National Trust Images / Robert Morris

Maps: Contain Ordnance Survey data
© Crown copyright and database right 2014

Ordnance Survey licence number 100039353

The information in this book has been produced in good faith and is intended as a general guide. Bradwell Books and its authors have made all reasonable efforts to ensure that the details are correct at the time of publication. Bradwell Books and the author cannot accept any responsibility for any changes that have taken place subsequent to the book being published. It is the responsibility of individuals undertaking any of the walks listed in this publication to exercise due care and consideration for the health and wellbeing of each other in the party. Particular care should be taken if you are inexperienced. The walks in this book are not especially strenuous but individuals taking part should ensure they are fit and able to complete the walk before setting off.

INTRODUCTION

THE PEAK DISTRICT NATIONAL PARK BROADLY DIVIDES INTO TWO DISTINCT AREAS, THE DARK PEAK AND THE WHITE PEAK.

The Dark Peak, most of which lies within the northern half of the National Park, is dominated by hills and moors, craggy escarpments called 'edges', rocky tors and deep valleys, some given over to reservoirs. When weathered, the coarse sandstone rock of this area, known as gritstone, grows dark in colour. In contrast, the southern half of the Peak District, the White Peak, is dominated by undulating upland with a scattering of prominent hills and deep, crag-lined river gorges. The rock here is limestone, which is grey-white in colour.

THE WALKS

The walks in this guide are evenly spread throughout the Peak District. All the routes follow rights of way or paths open to the public. Any road walking is along quiet lanes with little traffic. The walks should be suitable for most people, especially families, ranging in length from around two to six miles. They are also graded to help walkers select the most appropriate walk for the party.

WALK GRADES

1 – Any ascent is gradual
2 – Includes short, steeper climbs
3 – Includes more demanding climbs
4 – Includes more prolonged hill climbs.

ROUTE MAPS

The route map and directions accompanying each walk should be adequate to get you from start to finish but it is always advisable as a back-up to take the relevant Ordnance Survey map with you.

WHAT TO WEAR

I would strongly advise wearing walking boots. Given our unpredictable weather, a waterproof jacket and waterproof overtrousers are advised. Also, sufficient insulating clothing should be worn or carried that is appropriate to the time of year.

Refreshments

Possibilities for purchasing food and drink are given in 'The Basics' but are usually located at the start and end of walks. So something to drink and a snack are recommended additions to the rucksack.

Dogs

By law, dogs must be kept on a lead wherever there is livestock, and also in moorland areas during nesting season and where sheep roam freely. They should also be on a lead if they are likely to be a nuisance to other walkers or cyclists.

THIS VERY EASY WALK MEANDERS THROUGH ONE OF THE MOST PICTURESQUE VILLAGES IN THE COUNTRY AS WELL AS SAMPLING THE TISSINGTON TRAIL AND USING A FOOTPATH THROUGH MEADOWS THAT REVEAL ANCIENT PLOUGHING PATTERNS.

Tissington is an estate village of stone cottages centred on Tissington Hall, an early 17th-century Jacobean mansion house. The same family, the FitzHerberts, have lived here since they acquired the original moated manor in 1465 and continue to manage the estate. The parish church is the other dominant building in the village with a Norman tower and font.

Tissington is also well known for the annual well dressing. Six wells are decorated during the week of Ascension Sunday with pictures created by pressing flower petals, seeds and other organic materials into a clay base. The pictures usually, though not always, have a biblical theme. One of the most prominent of the wells is located opposite Tissington Hall. It is thought the origin of well dressing, now adopted by nearly every village in the Peak District, began at Tissington in 1348 following the village's escape from the Black Death. Villagers attributed this to the purity of water in its wells. Tissington gives its name to the Trail that passes through the village. Opened in 1971, the Tissington Trail, a footpath and

cycleway, is now part of the National Cycle Network. It runs for 13 miles from Parsley Hay in the north to Ashbourne in the south, following the course of the former railway line that connected Buxton to Ashbourne. The line enjoyed its heyday in the 1930s, when it was very popular with ramblers and other tourists.

The Walk

1. Leave the car park by the entrance, bear left, then turn right along The Foot. Follow this past cottages and a butcher's. Keep straight on after the last buildings – now Chapel Lane – as far as a fingerpost with footpaths going left and right at this point.

2. Turn right, pass through a squeeze stile and gate, cross a small field and exit by a gate on to another lane.

3. Turn right. Continue to where the tarmac ends at a bridge over the Tissington Trail.

THE BASICS

Distance: 2¾ miles / 4.2km
Gradients: No significant ascent or descent
Grade: 1
Approx. time to walk: Allow 1½ hours to 2 hours
Stiles: Two stone stiles
Path description: Village lanes, a trail and a field path
Maps: OS Explorer OL 24, White Peak Area
Start point: Tissington public car park. (GR SK 177 521)
Parking: As above (Postcode for Tissington Hall DE6 1RA)
Dog-friendly: Dogs on a lead where there is livestock and under close control on the Trail
Public toilets: Car park
Nearest food: Old Coach House Tearooms in village. Bluebell Inn on Buxton–Ashbourne road just west of village. Kiosk selling refreshments with picnic tables at car park

4. Do not cross the bridge. Instead, turn right, go through a gate and descend to the Tissington Trail, finishing with a few steps. Turn left, follow the Trail under the bridge, and continue for about three-quarters of a mile to where a footpath crosses the Trail. There is a particularly good view here of the rolling hills and deep valleys in this part of the White Peak.

5. Turn left for Tissington and climb the stile on the right of a gate. The path bears slightly right then becomes a walled track, which can be grassy or muddy dependent on the current state of the weather. Keep straight on and pass through a gate (or the stile on the left if it is locked). Notice the 'ridge and furrow' topography in the fields in the vicinity. This phenomenon was produced by a system of ploughing used in Europe during the Middle Ages. It was a result of ploughing with non-reversible ploughs on the same strip of land each year. Continue across another stone stile by a gate and join The Street. Follow this through the village past the impressive Tissington Hall and the lovely ornate well opposite.

6. Take a left fork in the road after the Old Coach House Tea Rooms, then bear left at the T-junction. Continue past the village pond, turning right into the car park.

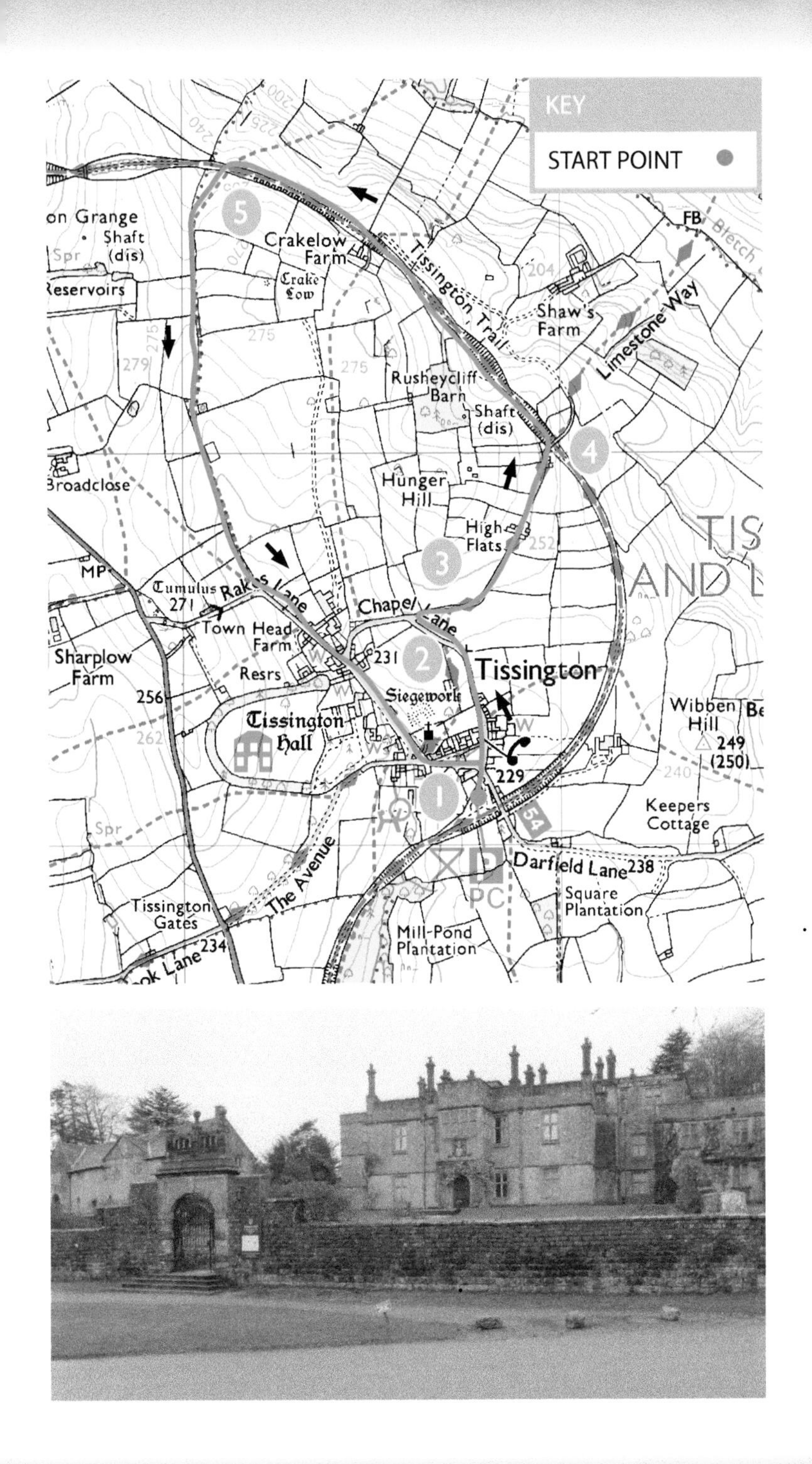
KEY
START POINT
Shaft
(dis)
Spr
Crakelow
Farm
Crake
Low
Tissington Trail
Shaw's
Farm
Limestone Way
FB
Rusheycliff
Barn
Shaft
(dis)
Broadclose
Hunger
Hill
High
Flats
MP
Tumulus
271
Rakes Lane
Chapel Lane
Town Head
Farm
Sharplow
Farm
Resrs
231
Siegeworks
Tissington
Tissington
Hall
Wibben
Hill
249
(250)
229
Keepers
Cottage
Darfield Lane
238
Square
Plantation
PC
Mill-Pond
Plantation
The Avenue
Tissington
Gates
234

WETTON

THIS WALK TAKES IN THE SPECTACULAR FEATURE OF THOR'S CAVE IN THE MANIFOLD VALLEY. FIELD PATHS, OLD GRASS TRACKS, AND THE TARMACKED MANIFOLD WAY ARE FOLLOWED, THEN A FOOTPATH WITH FLIGHTS OF STONE STEPS IS USED TO CLIMB THE STEEP VALLEY SIDE UP TO THE CAVE.

Wetton is an upland village of limestone cottages and farmhouses with a chapel, an inn, and a church with a 14th-century tower. Its history dates back to prehistoric times, and several 'lows' –burial mounds – in the locality point to occupation by Neolithic and Bronze Age settlers. In a chamber tomb on nearby Long Low the bones of thirteen individuals were found on excavation in 1849.

En route the footpath leads down to Wetton Mill in the Manifold Valley. The tearoom is the major draw these days and provides a welcome refreshment stop by the River Manifold for tourists walking or cycling along the Manifold Way. The hamlet takes its name from a building by the river that was a water-powered mill for grinding corn until the mid 19th century. It now belongs to the National Trust and is being restored as a museum piece. For much of the year the River Manifold becomes an underground river as it disappears through swallow holes in the riverbed just downstream from Wetton Mill, only to reappear further down the valley as it passes through the grounds of Ilam Hall.

As one rounds a bend along the Manifold Way, suddenly a gaping hole set high in a limestone cliff rising 300 feet from the valley bottom is revealed. This is Thor's Cave. The tough climb up to it is rewarded with a magnificent view from the mouth of the cave up the Manifold Valley. It is possible to explore the huge cavern but take care on the sloping, slippery, foot-polished limestone. Children should be closely supervised hereabouts. Excavations of the cave have produced human and animal bones, stone tools, pottery, amber beads and bronze items. The finds suggest the cavern was occupied from the Palaeolithic (Old Stone Age) through to the Roman period..

The Walk

1. Facing the road from the car park, turn left, then left at the junction ahead. Walk up through the village, passing Ye Olde Royal Oak. At the sharp, left-hand bend go straight ahead past Hill Farm Cottage. Follow the sign for Back of Ecton, keep

THE BASICS

Distance: 3¾ miles / 6km

Gradients: Steep climb out of the valley to Thor's Cave and just afterwards

Grade: 3

Approx. time to walk: Allow 2½ to 3 hours

Stiles: 4, of which 2 are very low wooden stiles

Path description: Several flights of stone steps up to Thor's Cave and a short, steep section along the concession path from the cave entrance

Map: OS Explorer Map OL24, The Peak District, White Peak Area

Start point: Wetton public car park. (GR SK 108 552)

Parking: Public car park in Wetton as above

Dog-friendly: On leads where there is livestock

Public toilets: Car park at Wetton

Nearest food: Ye Olde Royal Oak, Wetton. Teashop at Wetton Mill en route

straight on up the tarmac lane, and pass through a gateway and the squeeze stile straight ahead. Pass through a second squeeze stile with a small gate and enter the National Trust property of Wetton Hill. Cross two low wooden stiles.

2. After the second of these keep straight on as signposted to Ecton, ignoring the stone stile for Wetton Mill. Continue downhill with a wall on the left, and follow it as it bends left. Carry on downhill, cross a small stone footbridge, pass through a squeeze stile, then turn left in front of Pepper Inn cottage.

3. Pass through a gate and continue along the grass track down the winding valley to where it bends to the left, at which point there is a fingerpost indicating a public bridleway going right.

4. Follow the bridleway up a short rise and through a gate, then bear right as waymarked. Descend to Wetton Mill via a gate.

5. Cross the bridge, then follow the road signposted to Butterton for a few metres. Take the path on the left across a footbridge, then turn left to rejoin the road at the other side of a ford. Follow the quiet lane, which passes over a humpback bridge en route, to a road junction.

6. Turn sharp right to follow the Manifold Way. After half a mile Thor's Cave can be seen up to the left. Look for the footbridge down to the left at an information point.

7. Cross the footbridge and climb the steep footpath via steps and paving stones, turning right as signposted for Thor's Cave. The way up to the cave has a lot of steps. On arriving at the cave mouth pause to admire the view up the Manifold Valley. If exploring the cavern, take care on the sloping, polished rock. The walk continues uphill to the left of Thor's Cave. The first 50 metres requires care, especially in wet conditions. The path then levels out. Continue through a small gate and along the Concession Footpath as it descends slightly then climbs to a stile to the right of a gate.

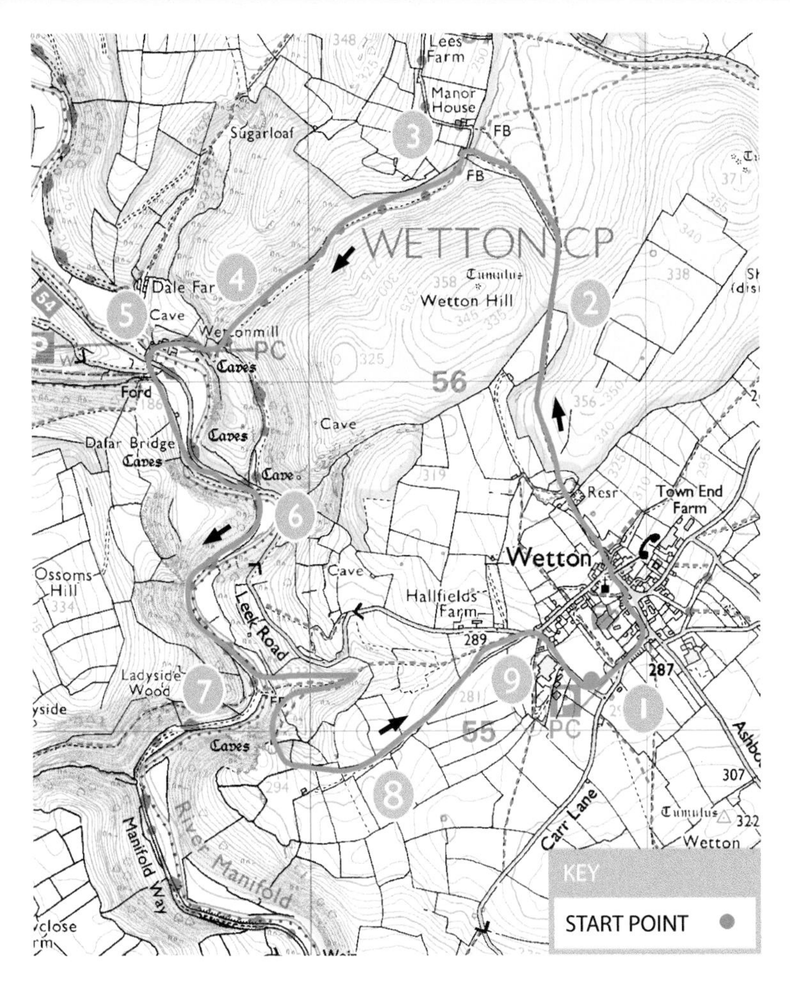

8. Cross the stile and turn left. Follow the track, cross another stile next to a gate, then continue to its junction with a road in Wetton.

9. Turn right, then left at the next road junction to finish.

THIS IS A LOW-LEVEL WALK AMIDST THE STUNNING HILL AND VALLEY SCENERY AROUND THE RIVER MANIFOLD, PASSING THROUGH OLD MINING AND MILL HAMLETS. A COMBINATION OF QUIET LANES, FOOTPATHS AND A SECTION OF THE MANIFOLD WAY ARE USED.

Hulme End is a small village that lies at the northern end of the Manifold Way, a tarmac walk and cycle path of nine miles through the beautiful winding valleys of the River Manifold and its tributary the River Hamps. The Manifold Way was originally the trackbed of the Leek and Manifold Valley Light Railway, which was narrow gauge and ran from Hulme End to Waterhouses from 1904 to 1934, when it closed down.

It carried both goods and passengers, the latter mainly for recreational use, and many of its passengers would have alighted at the station below Thor's Cave to visit this spectacular feature. Latterly, goods included milk that was shipped by rail to Finsbury Park in London from the creamery at Ecton a mile or so down the valley from Hulme End. The old station is currently a Visitor Centre.

At about the halfway point along the walk is Wetton Mill. This is a lovely and very popular spot at a bridge across the River Manifold with a tearoom and an old watermill that once ground corn. On the way back up the valley the Manifold Way passes the hamlet of Ecton at the bottom of Ecton Hill. Copper and lead deposits on Ecton Hill were worked from Bronze Age times to the late 19th century, a period of over 3,500 years. Once the richest and deepest copper, lead and zinc mines in Britain, the Ecton Mines are now a scheduled monument. In the 18th century the Duke of Devonshire, who owned Ecton Mines, made a profit of over £300,000. This was said to have financed the building of the magnificent Crescent in Buxton.

THE BASICS

Distance: 6 miles / 9.7km

Gradients: A mile of mostly gradual ascent on tarmac including one short, steep climb

Grade: 2

Approx. time to walk: Allow 3½ to 4 hours

Stiles: 2

Path description: Tarmac surfaces apart from ¾ mile on footpaths

Map: OS Explorer OL 24, Peak District, White Peak Area

Start point: Hulme End Visitor Centre and car park. (GR SK 102 593)

Parking: As above (Postcode SK17 0EZ)

Dog-friendly: On leads where there is livestock

Public toilets: Visitor Centre at Hulme End, and at Wetton Mill on route

Nearest food: Tea Junction tearoom adjacent to Visitor Centre and Manifold Inn at Hulme End. Teashop at Wetton Mill in season

1. Join the Manifold Way. Continue along the walk and cycleway for ¼ mile or so to a gate and stile on the left. Pass through the gate and walk straight ahead – no footpath in evidence – to the River Manifold, then bear left to a footbridge.

2. Cross the footbridge and join a minor road opposite Westside Mill, a private residence. Turn right and follow the road to a junction in 250 metres.

3. Turn left and follow the minor road signposted to Back of Ecton, which climbs gradually, passing to the right of an old mill pond. After a sharp right-hand bend the road climbs steeply for a short distance, then bends sharp left and continues climbing, mostly gradually, before levelling out, where a lane joins from the right. Keep straight on. Along this section the eye is drawn to the prominent steep-sided hills ahead with their smooth, sweeping flanks. These were once reef knolls in a tropical sea. The lane descends gradually at first, then drops steeply after a left-hand bend, passing a lovely cottage. Still on the road, continue round the right-hand bend and past Pepper Inn cottage, where the tarmac ends. Look at the inscription above the front door. Pass through a gate and continue for about half a mile down the winding valley along an old grassy track to where the valley bends left.

4. Bear right at the fingerpost and follow the bridleway up a short incline and through a gate. Bear right as waymarked down a stony and sometimes muddy path to a gate at the back of the hamlet of Wetton Mill. As you descend to the gate, a cave in a small cliff across the slope and easily accessed can be seen. This is worth exploring. Finds from the cave indicate that it was used as a rock shelter at various times in our prehistoric past.

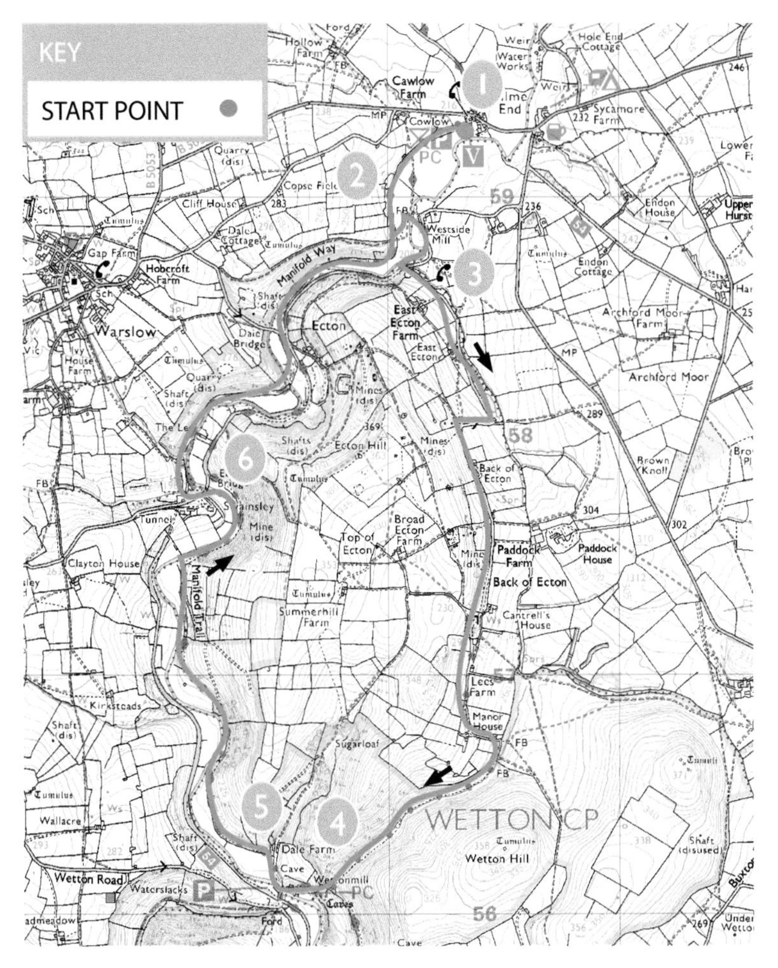

5. Pass in front of the teashop and, instead of crossing the bridge, keep straight on along a farm track. As you approach the farm, turn left as for Hulme End and pass through a gate. Follow the delightful old winding road for about a mile, where it joins a minor road after a gate.

6. Turn left, and follow the road across the bridge and uphill to where the Manifold Way crosses the road. The only tunnel along the Leek and Manifold Valley Light Railway is on the left at this point. Turn right opposite the tunnel and follow the Manifold Way back to Hulme End, crossing a minor road at Ecton en route.

HARTINGTON

THIS WALK FOLLOWS THE RIVER DOVE THROUGH A WINDING, WOODED GORGE THEN TAKES A HIGH-LEVEL ROUTE BACK ACROSS THE LIMESTONE PLATEAU WITH EXTENSIVE VIEWS OF THE AREA.

The starting point for the walk is Hartington, a tourist centre that can get very busy on summer weekends. Standing close to the River Dove, it is a village of attractive stone cottages and several splendid old buildings. The parish church of St Giles, in its dominating position on the flank of a hillside overlooking the village, dates from the 14th century. In the street below the church is the Old School House. And on the opposite side of the valley is Hartington Hall, a 17th century manor house where it is reputed Bonnie Prince Charlie stayed during the Jacobite rising of 1745. Nowadays it ranks as one of the grandest establishments owned by the Youth Hostel Association and has a café that is open to the public.

Another interesting building is the Old Hartington Cheese Shop, which sells an amazing variety of delicious cheeses. In the centre of the village one of the hostelries is named after Charles Cotton, who lived at Beresford Hall, a mile south of Hartington above the little wooded gorge of Beresford Dale. Cotton was a 17th-century poet and writer and contributed to his friend Izaak Walton's tome on fishing, The Compleat Angler. The original hall no longer exists as it fell into ruin but, almost hidden by trees at the top of the dale, Charles Cotton's Fishing House still survives. It was erected in 1674 and designed as a cosy base for his fishing exploits along the River Dove.

THE BASICS

Distance: 4 miles / 6.2km

Gradients: Any ascent is gradual apart from one short steep climb out of the dale

Grade: 2

Approx. time to walk: Allow 2½ to 3 hours

Stiles: None

Path description: Straightforward footpaths, a track and a tarmac lane

Map: OS Explorer OL 24, Peak District, White Peak Area

Start point: Market Place, Hartington. (GR SK 128 605)

Parking: Hartington public car park

Dog-friendly: On leads where there is livestock

Public toilets: Opposite car park entrance

Nearest food: Charles Cotton Hotel, Devonshire Arms, and three teashops/cafes

1. Walk past the Charles Cotton Hotel in the direction of the car park. Turn left at the public toilets. Pass just left of the building, go through a pedestrian gate and bear right along the footpath. Cross a track via two gates and follow the clear footpath. This descends and passes through an open gateway, climbs a little, then descends to a gate on the edge of a wood. Just before reaching this gate, Charles Cotton's Fishing House can be seen across the river. Continue through the wood and down to join the River Dove as it flows through Beresford Dale. The riverside path crosses the river at Pike's Pool, named after the pinnacle of limestone that stands on its own in the river like a large version of Excalibur. Continue downstream from here to another footbridge where a tarmac road meets the river.

2. Cross this footbridge, bear right, and then join the track on the left that runs parallel with the river. Follow this up to a metal gate and stile at a crossroads of tracks. Turn left here and follow the walled footpath uphill, steeply at first, to its junction with a lane.

3. Turn left and continue along the lane. This bends right after half a mile. Continue beyond this bend along the lane to a sharp left-hand bend.

4. Leave the lane at the bend and take the track going uphill signposted to Biggin and Heathcote. This joins another track at a T-junction in half a mile.

5. Turn left and follow this track over the brow of a hill and down to join a minor road.

6. Turn left and follow the road down into Hartington, passing 17th-century Hartington Hall en route. Turn left at the junction to finish.

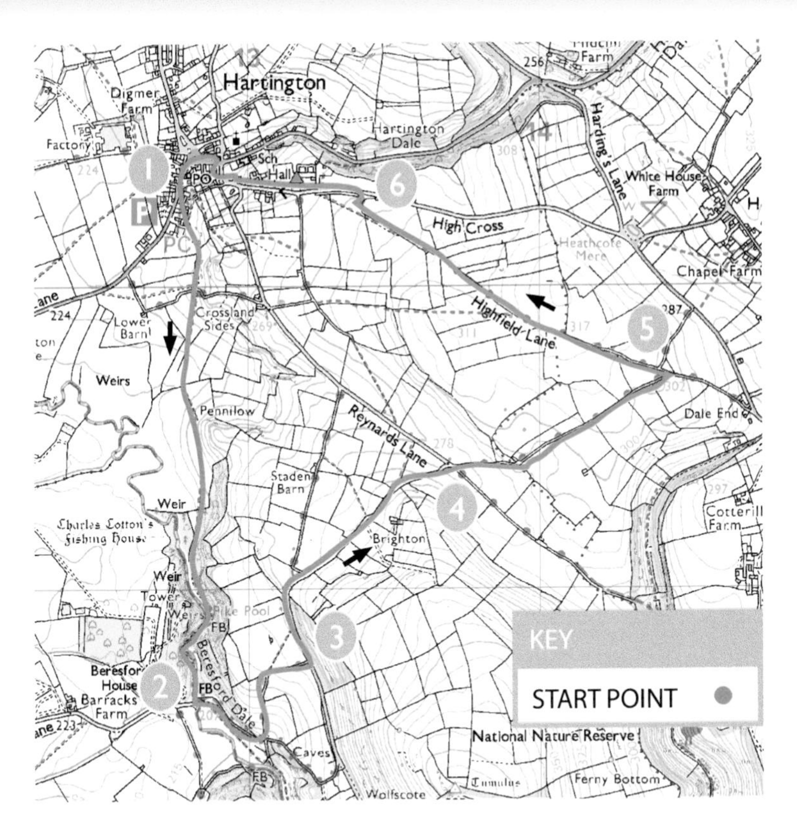
Hartington
Digmer Farm
Factory
Sch
Hall
PO
PC
Hartington Dale
High Cross
Harding's Lane
White House Farm
Heathcote Mere
Chapel Farm
Highfield Lane
Crossland Sides
Lower Barn
Weirs
Pennilow
Reynards Lane
Staden Barn
Dale End
Weir
Charles Cotton's Fishing House
Brighton
Cotterill Farm
Weir
Tower
Weirs
Pike Pool
FB
Beresford House
Barracks Farm
Beresford Dale
Caves
National Nature Reserve
Tumulus
Ferny Bottom
Wolfscote
KEY
START POINT

PILSBURY CASTLE

THE FIRST HALF OF THE WALK FOLLOWS A FOOTPATH OVERLOOKING THE DOVE VALLEY WITH FINE VIEWS OF THE AREA, THEN DESCENDS TO THE SITE OF A MEDIEVAL MOTTE AND BAILEY 'CASTLE', WHICH IS FUN TO EXPLORE. THE RETURN LEG IS ALONG A QUIET GATED LANE.

Pilsbury Castle is one of the most interesting medieval sites in the Peak District and is a scheduled ancient monument that can be freely explored. Built around a former limestone reef when this part of the earth's crust was submarine, one of several around the Dove Valley, the 'castle' includes a motte and two baileys, a typical 11th-century Norman fortress. The motte is clearly visible as a conical earthwork upon which a timber keep would have stood, with outer earthwork and timber defences enclosing the site. In all probability the castle was built on the site of a much earlier Iron Age fortification because of its location on the River Dove routeway near a crossing point on the river.

The nearby hamlet of Pilsbury was entered in the Domesday Book as being worth 10 shillings. Hartington, on the other hand, was given a value of 40 shillings! Hartington's medieval importance as a town was acknowledged in 1203, when the village was granted a charter to hold a weekly market, and has continued since that time to be the

major village of the central part of the Dove Valley. With a large market square and duck pond, fine old buildings that include a Norman Church and a 17th-century manor house, along with the fact that it is well supplied with hostelries and teashops, Hartington nowadays is a magnet for tourists to the area.

THE BASICS

Distance: 5¼ miles / 8.5km

Gradients: Gradual apart from one short, steep grassy descent

Grade: 2

Approx time to walk: Allow 3½ to 4 hours

Stiles: Five, but only one that might be challenging to some

Path description: Straightforward field paths with occasional short muddy sections and a tarmac lane

Map: OS Explorer Map OL24, The Peak District, White Peak Area

Start point: Hartington Market Place. (GR SK 128 605)

Parking: Public car park, Hartington

Dog-friendly: On leads where there is livestock

Public toilets: Opposite the car park

Nearest food: 2 pubs and 3 cafes/teashops in Hartington

1. Walk past the large duck pond away from Market Place. Continue along the road, which becomes a gated lane. In just over half a mile pass through the gate adjacent to Bank Top Farm.

2. Turn right to go up the concrete track opposite the farm. At the right-hand hairpin bear left through a gate to follow the waymarked footpath. Continue along the footpath highlighted with blue painted posts. There are particularly good views of the valley in both directions along this section of the walk – north to the prominent pointed Chrome Hill, and south to the hills around Dove Dale. After crossing a wooden stile the field ahead has several mounds. These are spoil heaps from lead mining. There are a number of capped mineshafts here. Continue along the well-marked footpath, following the signs for Pilsbury/ Crowdecote. The path bears right at the top of a rise to a stone stile.

3. Cross this then head down the steep grass slope as signposted to Pilsbury/ Crowdecote to a path junction.

4. Turn left and continue to a minor road via a wooden stile. Cross the road and join the path opposite via a gate, then bear slightly left. Continue through another gate, then an open gap in the wall ahead left of a stile. Continue straight on. After crossing another wooden stile there is a good view of the motte and bailey on which Pilsbury Castle once stood. Interestingly, the shape of the limestone outcrop that formed part of the defensive wall echoes the distant peak of Chrome Hill. Descend to the track below and enter the compound to explore Pilsbury Castle.

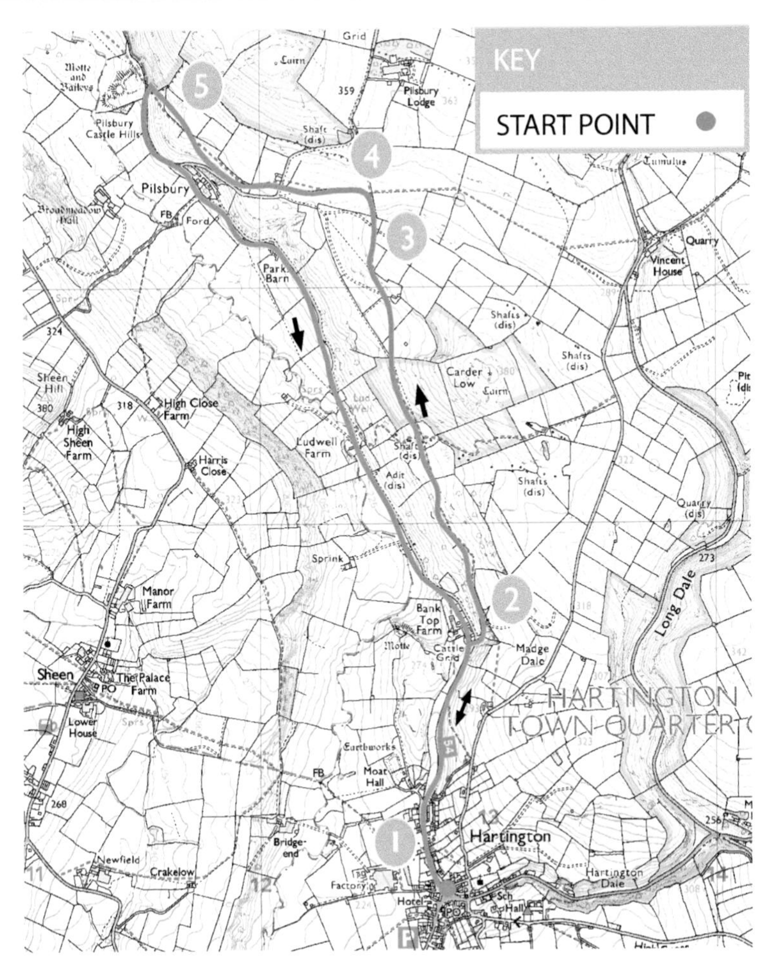

5. Return to the gate of the compound, then turn right to walk south down the valley towards Hartington. Follow the grassy track through two gates, then bear right to continue down the valley on the tarmac lane, passing the tiny hamlet of Pilsbury en route. The lane leads back to Hartington.

OVER HADDON

Starting at an upland White Peak village, the first half of the walk descends to one of the most attractive of the Peak District's limestone dales to follow the riverside path past numerous weirs and pools.

The walk starts at Over Haddon, a quiet little village to the south*west of Bakewell perched above Lathkill Dale, from which there are extensive views of the surrounding hills and limestone dales. The village has some delightful old stone cottages and an 18th-century hostelry, the Lathkill Hotel, known as the Miner's Arms until 1896.

Over Haddon has a strong association with lead mining, and the central part of Lathkill Dale, just down from the village, has many relics of this past industry, including the ruins of the engine house of Mandale Mine. In 1854 the 'Lathkill Gold Rush' began when 'gold' was struck at a mine in the dale. This soon fizzled out, however, when it was discovered the 'gold' was, in fact, iron pyrites or 'fools' gold'.

At the halfway point along the walk is Alport, an attractive hamlet of 17th and 18th-century stone cottages at an ancient crossing point on the River Bradford. It also has an old water-powered former corn mill that can be seen just downstream of the old packhorse bridge. Although the present building probably dates from the 18th century, a corn mill was recorded here as long ago as 1159. Alport lies on the 'Portway', which it is thought was one of the most important prehistoric roads in the area. The village was probably a trading post in Roman times.

THE BASICS

Distance: 4 miles, 6km

Gradients: Apart from a steep tarmac lane out of Alport, all ascent is gradual

Grade: 3

Approx. time to walk: Allow 2½ to 3 hours

Stiles: Three

Path description: A combination of riverside footpaths with short muddy sections after wet weather, and field paths

Map: OS Explorer Map OL24, The Peak District, White Peak Area

Start point: Over Haddon car park. (GR SK 203 664)

Parking: Over Haddon car park. Postcode DE45 1JE

Dog-friendly: Dogs on a lead where there is livestock

Public toilets: Car park at Over Haddon

Nearest food: Lathkill Hotel at Over Haddon

1. Exit the car park on the right of the toilet block, signposted Lathkill Dale, then descend the steep zigzag lane to the River Lathkill.

2. Turn left along the riverside footpath. This climbs a little at a rocky section, after which it passes above the crystal-clear river as it runs through a gorge and drops over numerous weirs. The path emerges at a road on the left of an ancient, narrow bridge, medieval Conksbury Bridge.

3. Turn right, cross the bridge and continue up the narrow lane. As this bends right, the levelled areas in the field on the right formed the platforms upon which houses of the medieval village of Conksbury once stood. On the left of the lane opposite is a footpath with fingerpost. Continue downstream along this footpath, now on the right of the river. Further on, the path crosses a track. Keep straight on along the footpath to emerge at the road that runs through the tiny village of Alport.

4. Cross the road with care, go left, then almost immediately right down the narrow lane between cottages. The lane bends round to the left between cottages and delightful riverside gardens, then meets another minor road at a T-junction. The arched bridge just to the right is another ancient bridge. Looking downstream from the bridge the old building on the right bank was once a water-powered corn mill.

5. Turn left. Walk up to the main road crossed a little earlier. Cross this with care and climb the steep tarmac lane opposite. This is the 'Portway', a road that has been in existence since prehistoric times. Keep straight on to where it levels out and arrives at a barn. The tarmac ends here and the continuation track can be muddy in the vicinity of the barn after wet weather. Continue through the farmyard to a gate on the left with yellow and blue waymarkers and a fingerpost.

6. Pass through this gate, then bear half right across the large field as signposted to Over Haddon. Cross a stile and the field beyond to arrive at a minor road via a small gate. Cross the road and the squeeze stile opposite, then keep straight on. After passing through another gate there is a stunning view of Lathkill Dale and its numerous weirs below – a great picnic spot. Keep straight on, pass through a gate on the right as directed, then bear left up the field. Pass through gates and another field to emerge adjacent to the Lathkill Hotel.

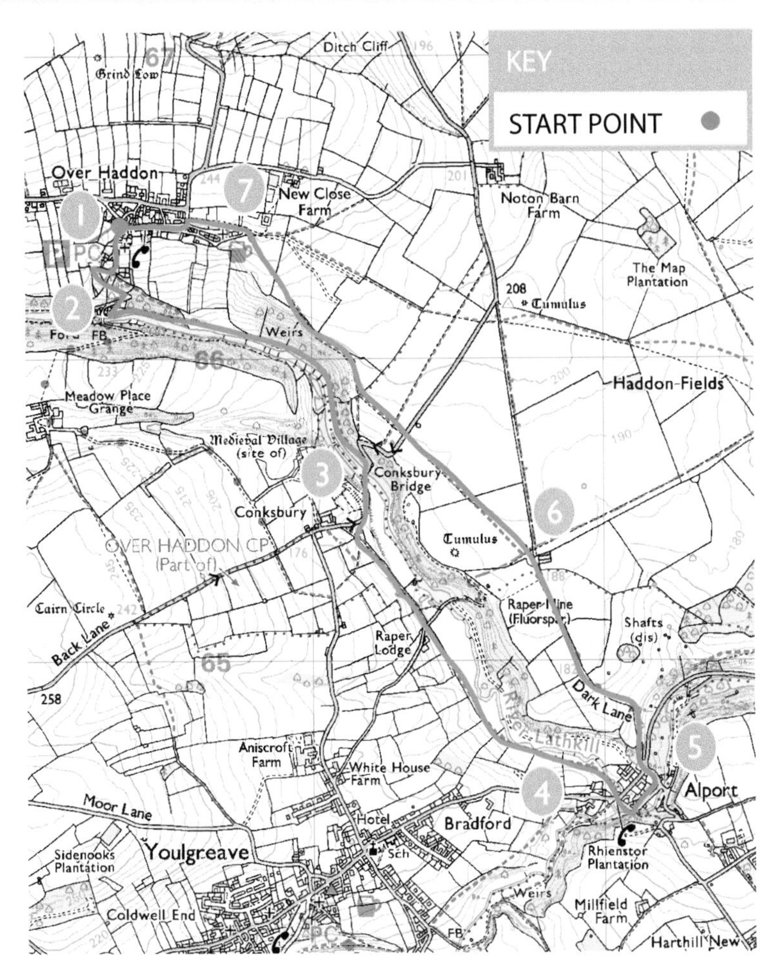

7. Pass in front of the hotel, then bear left at a fork. Follow the lane down past the old village water pump and up to join a higher road, where you bear left to the car park.

CHATSWORTH WOODS

A COMBINATION OF TARMAC LANES, TRACKS AND FOOTPATHS TAKE YOU THROUGH THE EXOTIC AND FASCINATING STAND WOODS ON THE HILLSIDE ABOVE CHATSWORTH HOUSE. LAKES, A GIANT ROCKERY AND SEVERAL WATER FEATURES ENSURE A VARIED OUTING.

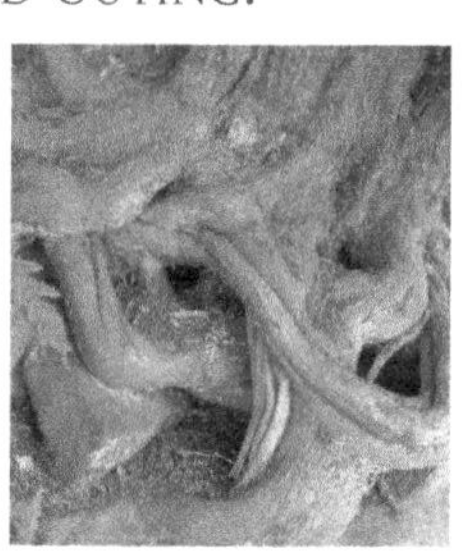

Chatsworth is the seat of the Duke of Devonshire and has been home to the Cavendish family since Bess of Hardwick settled here in 1549. The present stately home's construction was begun in 1687, and the naturalistic setting for the house was the creation of landscape architect Lancelot 'Capability' Brown in the 18th century for the 4th Duke.

The more adventurous route to the Hunting Tower described takes you past several features that were the creation of the 6th Duke and his head gardener Joseph Paxton in the 19th century. These include the aquaduct with its waterfall, and the tumbling stream that begins at a waterfall on the crest of the hillside. The woodland footpaths wind amongst rocky outcrops of gritstone and an amazing variety of mature and exotic broad-leaved and coniferous trees, which lend a mysterious atmosphere to the woods.

The footpath followed leads to the Hunting Tower, built around 1582 as a summerhouse for Bess of Hardwick, and now available for rent as holiday accommodation. The view from the front of the tower over Chatsworth is quite magnificent. The three iron cannon are genuine museum pieces and are reputed to have come from one of the ships in Nelson's fleet that fought at the Battle of Trafalgar.

Further along, the walk passes first Emperor Lake, which supplies the water that produces the Emperor Fountain in the grounds of Chatsworth House, then Swiss Lake, with Swiss Cottage on the far bank.

THE BASICS

Distance: 3½ miles / 5.6km

Gradients: A steep climb at the start

Grade: 2

Approx time to walk: Allow 2 to 2½ hours

Stiles: None

Path description: Choice of just tarmac lanes and tracks or with the addition of some woodland paths where steps are encountered

Map: OS Explorer OL24, The Peak District, White Peak Area

Start point: Chatsworth House. (GR SK 260 703)

Parking: Main car park (fee payable) Postcode DE45 1PP

Dog-friendly: Dogs should be on a lead

Public toilets: Several close to the car park

Nearest food: Cavendish Rooms and other refreshment possibilities

1. From the car park walk uphill as for the Farmyard and Adventure Playground. On the approach to the Farmyard go through the pedestrian gate on the right signposted Stand Wood. Continue up the tarmac lane. For the easiest option to reach the Hunting Tower stay on the lane as far as a junction with another tarmac lane, then turn left to follow this up to the Tower.

2. A more adventurous route is to turn left as signposted to The Dell 150 metres or so uphill of the Farmyard. Follow this up to the tarmac lane mentioned above. Cross this and continue straight on up the footpath and wooden steps with views of the aqueduct and waterfall. Stay on the main footpath as it zigzags steeply uphill on the right of the tumbling stream. The last part of the ascent climbs stone steps to the top of a waterfall. Small children need close supervision hereabouts. Pause to take in the fine view down the watercourse to Chatsworth House and Edensor beyond.

3. Now descend stone steps on the other side of the waterfall, then continue on this level, ignoring steps descending to the left, past unusual rock formations and through fairytale woodland, eventually arriving at the 16th-century Hunting Tower. Take a moment to absorb the striking view from the front of the Tower.

4. Facing the front of the Tower, pass it on the right and keep straight on along an earth track, which soon joins a gravel track coming from the left.

5. Turn right here. Follow the main track, ignoring any other possibilities. This passes the top of Emperor Lake and, a little further on, Swiss Lake, easily identifiable by the chalet-like Swiss Cottage on the far bank of the lake. Stay on the main track, which forks right at a junction. Eventually a crossroads is reached.

6. Either turn right and follow the tarmac lane, via a zigzag, all the way back down to Chatsworth House, at any junctions taking the downhill option. Or a more interesting route is to go straight across at the junction as signposted to Hob's

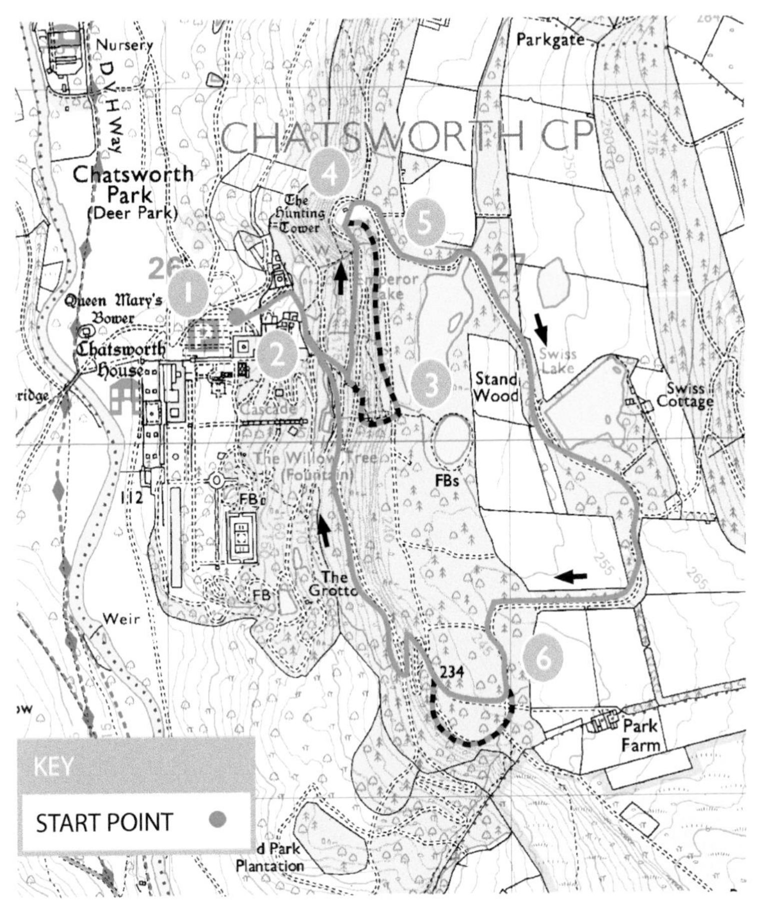

House and Beeley but where the track bends sharp left go straight on along a little-used grassy footpath. This bends right shortly and joins the tarmac lane in about 300 metres, passing through some ancient woodland on the way. Bear left on joining the lane and continue as above.

View of Chatsworth House Bridge

Beautiful house at Edensor

CHATSWORTH PARK

THIS IS A WALK ALONG TRACKS AND FIELD PATHS, PASSING THROUGH SHEEP AND DEER PASTURE AMIDST THE ROLLING, TREE-FLECKED LANDSCAPE OF CHATSWORTH PARK, AND FINISHING WITH A STRETCH ALONGSIDE THE RIVER DERWENT.

The walk starts above the River Derwent near Chatsworth Garden Centre at Calton Lees. The park was landscaped by Lancelot 'Capability' Brown in the 18th century, and the tree flecked pastures on both sides of the river is the impressive result. The 4th Duke wanted to create a man-made setting for the house that gave the illusion of natural countryside.

The route used from Calton Lees climbs to and crosses a broad ridge. After passing through a strip of woodland the walk arrives at a point with benches. These are provided so that visitors can sit down to appreciate what is probably the best view of Chatsworth House in its setting by the river, backed by the tree-covered slope of Stand Wood.

A descent through pasture, where red and fallow deer are frequently seen amidst the sheep, leads to the estate village of Edensor. The village was originally located close to the River Derwent below Chatsworth House. This was razed and later rebuilt in the 19th century by the 6th Duke of Devonshire and his Kew Gardens-trained head gardener, Joseph Paxton.

Further along and just across the river is the strange structure known as Queen Mary's Bower. This was built by Bess of Hardwick as a feature within water gardens that surrounded the original Elizabethan manor. It takes its name from Mary, Queen of Scots, who was imprisoned at Chatsworth on several occasions before her final demise. The ruin near the end of the walk was a water-powered mill that ground corn for animal feed until 1952, when it closed down. It was badly damaged in the great gale of 1962, when two beech trees fell on it.

THE BASICS

Distance: 4 miles / 6km

Gradients: Apart from a short, steep zigzag, the first 1½ miles is a gradual climb

Grade: 2

Approx. time to walk: Allow 2½ to 3 hours

Stiles: None

Path description: Straightforward on a combination of tracks and field paths

Map: OS Explorer OL24, The Peak District, White Peak Area

Start point: Calton Lees Car Park near Chatsworth Garden Centre. (GR SK 258 685)

Parking: As above (fee payable) Postcode DE4 2NX

Dog-friendly: On leads where there is livestock

Public toilets: Garden Centre adjacent to car park

Nearest food: The Vines Restaurant and Coffee Shop at the Garden Centre

1. From the car park walk in the direction of the Garden Centre, then continue straight on along the tarmac lane. This bends right and comes to a gate with a horseshoe sign. Pass through the gate and continue uphill along the gravel track. Part way up an attractive spring with a horse trough hewn out of local sandstone is passed. The sandstone is known as millstone grit, and it is the rock that forms the crags of the long 'edges' that stretch for miles from the Upper Derwent Valley south through Chatsworth Estate and beyond. Eventually, the track does a steep zigzag to outlying cottages and a ruined barn awaiting restoration. Continue past the cottages, still climbing, to a gate.

2. Bear right after the gate for another short uphill stretch before level ground is reached. Continue towards the wood ahead, then go through a gate and follow the track downhill, exiting from the wood by another gate or stile. From here there is a magnificent view of Chatsworth House in the valley below, and the Hunting Tower can be picked out high in the woods behind the House.

3. Continue straight down the hillside. Pass left of a small, fenced wood then maintain the same direction, heading just left of the church spire. As you near the back of cottages in Edensor look for the waymark post and the little iron gate, which is to the right of the blue wooden one. Pass through this then descend a flight of stone steps to the road in the village.

4. Turn right and walk through Edensor, passing beneath the imposing church and attractive cottages. Continue down to the main road, cross it with care, and follow the gravel footpath. This climbs a little, then descends to the bridge across the River Derwent. Cross the bridge, pausing to admire the view of Chatsworth House and the river, then bear left through a gate to visit the squat stone tower known as Queen Mary's Bower, the main visual remnant of the original Elizabethan garden.

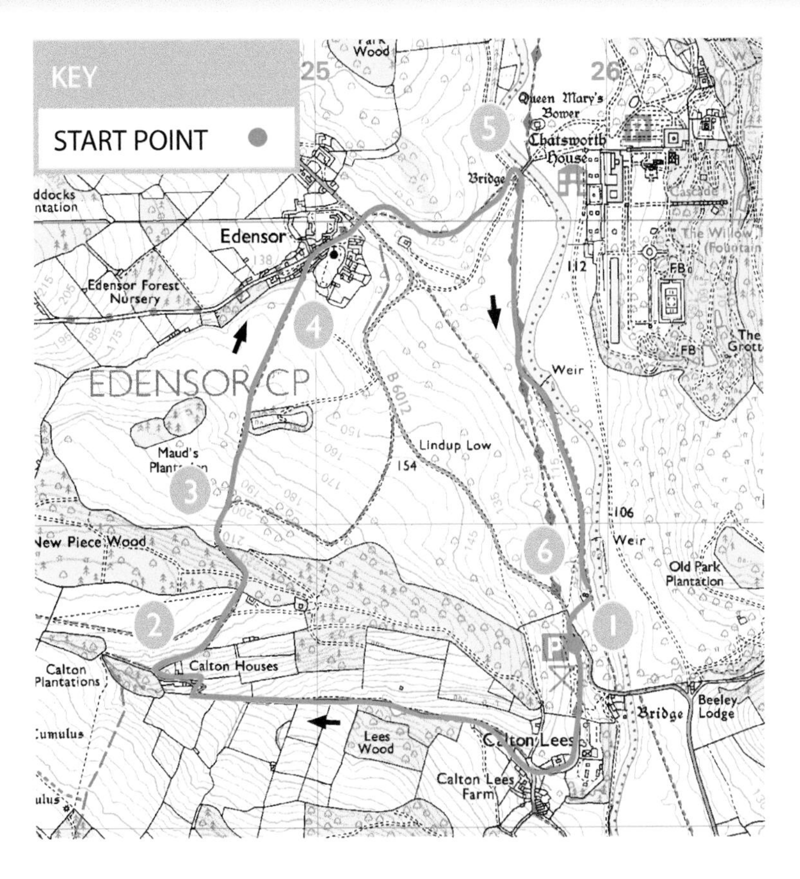

5. Retrace your steps across the bridge, then bear left across the riverside meadow. In wet conditions, the drier option is to stay close to the river bank. The path climbs a little at a river bend then descends and regains the riverside. Continue as far as the ruined corn mill.

6. Turn right immediately after passing the ruin and head straight up, steeply, to the road at the cattle grid. Cross the road with care, go through the blue pedestrian gate and so back to the car park.

BASLOW

USING TRACKS AND FOOTPATHS A CLIMB FROM BASLOW IN STAGES LEADS UP TO A VIEWPOINT OVERLOOKING THE DERWENT VALLEY, THEN LEVEL WALKING ALONG THE TOP OF BASLOW EDGE LEADS TO ANOTHER VIEWPOINT CLOSE TO WELLINGTON'S MONUMENT. THE DESCENT FOLLOWS AN ANCIENT 'ROAD' BACK TO THE VILLAGE.

Baslow is a sprawling though attractive village at the northern end of Chatsworth Park. It is made up of five 'Ends': Far, Nether, Bridge, West and Over Ends. The oldest part of the village is Bridge End, clustered around the Church of St Anne near the bridge. The church has an unusual clock, for on its face 'Victoria 1897' is inscribed instead of numbers. The beautiful arched bridge was built in 1603 and has a tiny stone toll house just big enough for the toll keeper to shelter in.

The most visited part of Baslow is Nether End. This is partly due to the existence of a pedestrian entrance to Chatsworth Park here but also because of the concentration of hotels, pubs, restaurants and a teashop overlooking the village green.

On our route, after walking above Baslow Edge, the walk passes close to a large block of weathered gritstone known as the Eaglestone. In the past it was the custom for young men of Baslow to make the difficult climb up the Eaglestone to demonstrate their fitness for the responsibilities of marriage. There are no easy ways up it!

Nearby is Wellington's Monument. This was erected in 1866 by a Lieutenant Colonel E.M. Wrench of Baslow to commemorate a visit by the Duke of Wellington to the moor. It was also intended to complement Nelson's Monument above the crags of Birchen Edge across the valley. In the past there would have been a view from the monument across to Chatsworth House and Gardens but trees now obstruct this.

THE BASICS

Distance: 4 miles / 6.4km

Gradients: Steep initial climb out of Baslow, then more gradual climbs on first half of walk

Grade: 3

Approx. time to walk: Allow 3 to 3½ hours

Stiles: 1 ladder stile

Path description: Path below Baslow Edge is muddy in parts after wet weather. Otherwise straightforward tracks and paths.

Map: OS Explorer Map OL24, The Peak District, White Peak Area

Start point: Pay-and-Display car park at Baslow. (GR SK 258 722)

Parking: Pay-and-Display car park at Baslow

Dog-friendly: Dogs on a lead where there is livestock

Public toilets: Car park at Baslow

Nearest food: Café on The Green and several pubs in the village

1. On leaving the car park, cross the main road at the pedestrian crossing then bear left up Eaton Hill. Continue to where the road bends left, then turn right up Bar Road. The road degenerates into a track and gets steeper. Climb as far as the right-hand bend, where there is a gate and squeeze stile on the left.

2. Pass through the stile and continue along a more gradually ascending grassy track. If you look across the Derwent Valley along this section, you will see in large letters 'ER' as a planted arrangement of shrubs on a sloping hillside. This was created to commemorate the coronation of the present Queen Elizabeth. After crossing a ladder stile on the left of a gate a gravel track is joined. Follow this until it turns sharply uphill by a wall. Instead, keep straight ahead alongside the wall on the left. After passing through a gate, take the path down to the left, ignoring other options, and continue for 100 metres to a signpost at a path crossroads.

3. Go straight across and continue as for Curbar Edge. The footpath more or less contours the hillside below Baslow Edge. This can be muddy in parts after wet weather. Eventually, after passing through a gate, another path crossroads is reached.

4. Turn right to follow the path uphill, climbing a few steps before bearing left to join a minor road via another gate. Either turn right and walk with care along the roadside up to gates on the right or, a safer option with children, take the narrow path by the wall to the same point.

5. After passing through one of the gates on the right, follow the main footpath for a few metres then turn right to visit

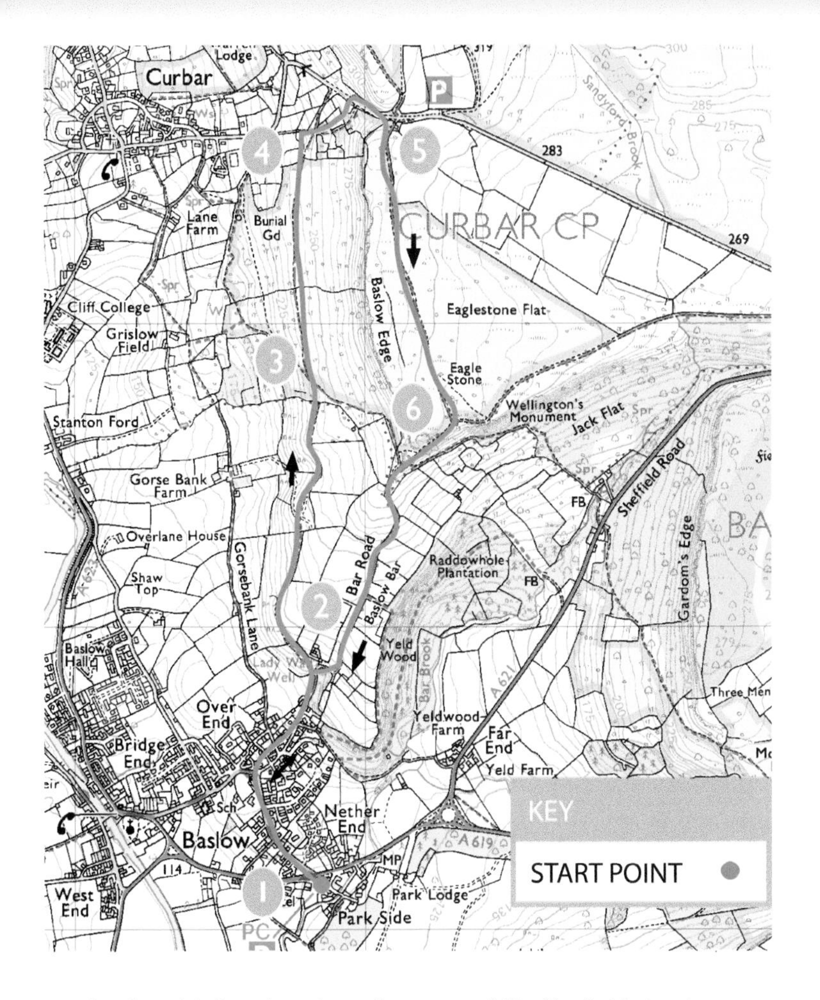

the viewpoint. From here, two options are available. The first is to retrace your steps to the main footpath and turn right to follow it across the moor. A much more interesting option is to bear left from the viewpoint and follow the little-used path along the top of Baslow Edge as it winds its way amongst rocks with fine views of the Derwent Valley. Both paths lead to the same path junction near Wellington's Monument.

6. Turn right at this point – or keep straight on if returning to the path junction from the monument. Follow the track downhill, passing through a gate. The track is Bar Road, used on the ascent, and descends to Baslow. Bear left along Eaton Hill to return to the car park.

ASHFORD-IN-THE-WATER

THIS WALK STARTS IN A PICTURESQUE VILLAGE OF STONE COTTAGES ON THE RIVER WYE. A STEADY BUT GRADUAL CLIMB ALONG FOOTPATHS LEADS UP TO THE POPULAR VIEWPOINT AT MONSAL HEAD.

Ashford-in-the-Water grew up at a fording point on the River Wye. It was entered in the Domesday Book as 'Aisseford', and the tearoom has taken its name from the Old English name for the village. The packhorse bridge known as Sheepwash Bridge has spanned the river near the location of the ford since the early 17th century. Until fairly recent times sheep were brought here to be washed before being sheared. The ewes, with halters round their necks, were penned in the walled enclosure adjacent to the bridge. They were then pushed into the river, ducked and made to swim downstream to rejoin their lambs on the riverbank.

Ashford is known for its 'Black Marble'. Towards the end of the 19th century a local industry developed around the mining of a dark limestone on the edge of the village.

This turned jet black when polished and was in demand as an ornamental stone. The village is also known for the 'Maiden's Garlands' made to mark the deaths of virgins until 1801. Some of these are preserved in the parish church, which dates from the 12th century, although much remodelling has taken place over the centuries. Also of interest, the base and stump of a 15th-century market cross lie in the churchyard.

En route is the pretty little hamlet of Little Longstone, which has a 16th-century inn, a 17th-century Manor House and a delightful Victorian chapel. A little further on is the famous viewpoint at Monsal Head with its ice cream vendors, café and hotel.

THE BASICS

Distance: 4 miles / 6.4km

Gradients: Apart from the initial climb out of Ashford, any ascent is gradual

Grade: 2

Approx. time to walk: Allow 3 to 3½ hours

Stiles: Several but only two attain the full height of a wall

Path description: Occasional muddy parts after wet spells. For a short distance beyond Monsal Head the footpath crosses a steep, wooded slope.

Map: OS Explorer Map OL24, The Peak District, White Peak area

Start point: Sheepwash Bridge. (GR SK 194 696)

Parking: Either in Ashford public car park or between the church and Sheepwash Bridge

Dog-friendly: On leads where there is livestock

Public toilets: Car park

Nearest food: Aisseford Tearooms, Bulls Head, Ashford Arms. Also at Monsal Head

1. From Sheepwash Bridge walk up Fennel Street. At the left-hand bend bear right up Vicarage Lane. At the top of the incline keep straight ahead along the lane for another 100 metres to a squeeze stile with fingerpost on the right soon after the sign to Monsal Head.

2. Go through the stile, cross a small field and the stile ahead which leads directly on to a busier road. Cross this with care and take the path almost opposite signposted to Monsal Head. Follow the gated footpath as it descends, then climbs a little and continues to a minor road. Cross this and the gated stile opposite. Follow the footpath up through several fields with gated stiles. Eventually, stone steps are reached in a retaining wall for the Monsal Trail.

3. Cross the Trail and take the path signposted to Little Longstone via a stile. The path continues up through several fields with gates and arrives at the road that runs through Little Longstone. Opposite at this point is the 17th-century Manor House.

4. Turn left and walk along the pavement past the Packhorse Inn, which has a sign that says 'Muddy boots, kids and dogs are welcome'! After passing a row of pretty cottages adorned with flowers you pass the Victorian chapel, which was built around 1870. A quarter of a mile further on the pavement ends at Monsal Head. Cross the main road with care and head for the viewpoint at the front of the Monsal Head Hotel. This is a popular spot with tourists because of the stunning view of Monsal Dale and the availability of various refreshments in this vicinity!

5. Facing the view, turn left and head for a gap in the wall just beyond Hobb's Café. Pass through the gap and turn left to follow the footpath signposted to Ashford and Monsal Dale. After a few metres in descent, take the left fork as

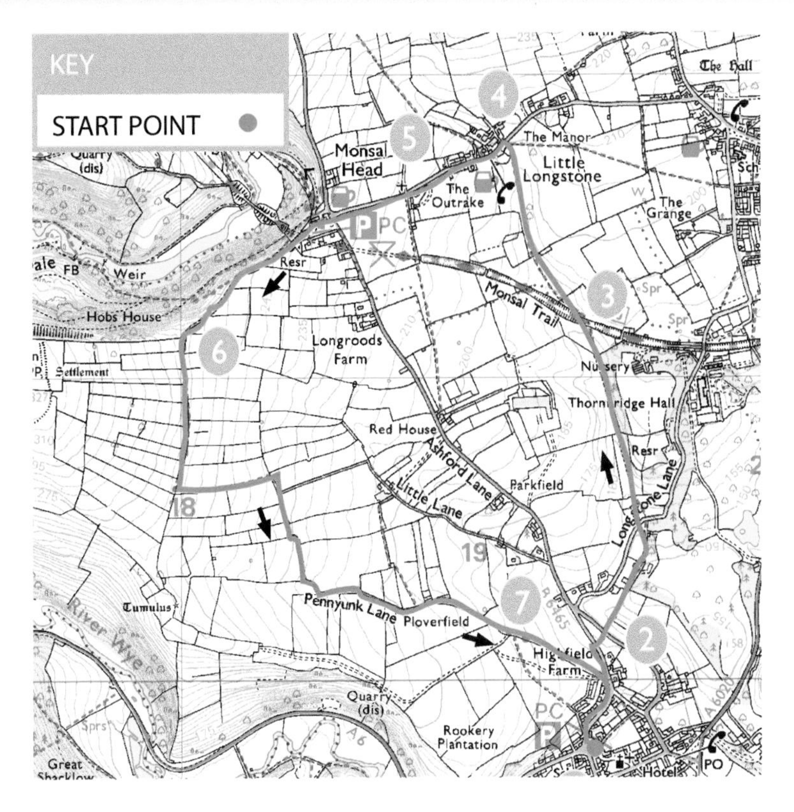

signposted to Ashford. This begins as a narrow footpath along a steep, wooded slope, then climbs a few steps before developing into a wider path. Continue to a post with waymark arrows.

6. Bear left at the yellow waymark along the walled and gated footpath. Up to the right is Fin Cop, the site of a Bronze Age fort where significant archaeological finds have been excavated. Keep to the waymarked route, which turns sharp left at a gate and descends a large field before turning right at another gate to resume the former direction. At a footpath junction further on, keep straight on. The footpath eventually becomes a wider track and descends to the top of Vicarage Lane used at the beginning of the walk.

7. Turn right, walk down the lane, then bear left down Fennel Street back to Sheepwash Bridge.

MONSAL HEAD

A WALK WITH STUNNING VIEWS AND 19TH-CENTURY RAILWAY ARCHITECTURE PASSING THROUGH A LIMESTONE GORGE WITH A RIVER RUNNING THROUGH. A COMBINATION OF FOOTPATHS, A HIGH-LEVEL TRACK AND THE MONSAL TRAIL ARE USED, AND THERE ARE TWO STIFF CLIMBS UP WOODED HILLSIDES.

The walk starts at Monsal Head, which draws many tourists for the exceptionally fine view of Monsal Dale, a river gorge with a former railway track running through it. The tortuous route through the gorge, built by the Midland Railway as a scenic attraction, demanded several tunnels and the building of the impressive Headstone Viaduct, better known as the Monsal Viaduct. The railway line ran from 1863 to 1968, and the trackbed is now the very popular Monsal Trail.

The Monsal Head Hotel, formerly the Railway Hotel when the line was in use, would have been a popular stopping-off point for the Victorian visitor, who would have alighted at Upperdale in the valley and been conveyed by horse-drawn carriage up to the hotel. The River Wye was important during the Industrial Revolution as it powered the cotton mills of Litton and Cressbrook upstream of Monsal Head.

After the winding climb through the woods to the farm at Brushfield Hough, there is plenty of opportunity to take in one's glorious surroundings. Across the river and dominating the valley is Fin Cop, a hill with steep flanks and earthworks created during the Later Bronze Age. Longstone Local History Group have carried out extensive research of the hillfort. Excavations during 2009 and 2010 produced some finds from a mass grave that included the skulls of females and infants. Barrows and round-house platforms were also found, suggesting this was a major settlement during the Bronze and Iron Ages.

THE BASICS

Distance: 4 miles / 6.4km

Gradients: Includes a gradual descent into the valley, and two steep climbs on woodland paths

Grade: 3

Approx. time to walk: Allow 3 to 3½ hours

Stiles: One

Path description: Footpaths and tracks with short muddy sections after wet weather

Map: OS Explorer Map OL24, The Peak District, White Peak Area

Start point: Viewpoint in front of Monsal Head Hotel. (GR SK 185 715)

Parking: Monsal Head pay-and-display car park, Postcode DE45 1NL

Dog-friendly: On leads where there is livestock

Public toilets: Monsal Head

Nearest food: Stables Bar and Hobb's Café at Monsal Head

1. The walk is described from the viewpoint overlooking the spectacular gorge of Monsal Dale. Facing the dale, go left to the fingerpost just beyond the café, and turn left to follow the narrow path signposted Ashford and Monsal Dale. In a short distance the path forks. Take the right fork and follow the descending footpath through woodland, meeting the River Wye at a large and beautiful weir. Cross the river by the footbridge.

2. Turn left and take the path following the river downstream. Either stay on this or take short diversions to follow the riverside. The main footpath gets muddy in parts after a prolonged wet spell. Continue down the dale for about a kilometre to a fingerpost on the right.

3. Turn right for Brushfield Hough and follow the steep, zigzag path up through woods. Eventually, the ground levels off, and the path arrives at a stile in a stone wall.

4. Cross this and bear right along the track that leads to farm buildings. On approaching the buildings bear left off the track to a gate. Pass through this and bear left between farm buildings, go through another gateway, then turn right to follow the farm track. Continue through a gate. After the second gateway bear slightly right along a field path and continue to a track.

5. Turn right, go through a gate, and follow the high-level track, taking short diversions on the right of the track in wet conditions. On the opposite side of the valley the great bulk of Fin Cop can be seen, and clear traces of ancient footpaths can be picked out leading from the

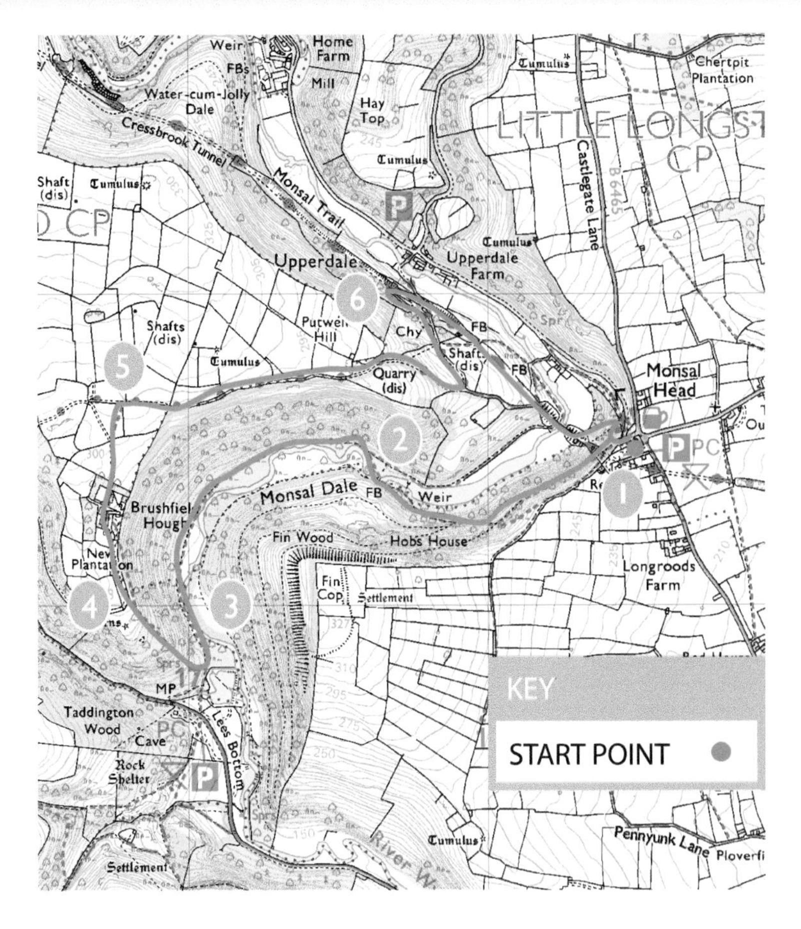

hilltop to the river. Eventually, the track begins to descend after passing a relic of the lead-mining industry. The descent is best taken on the right of the track, which is stony and awkward. Follow the track around a left-hand bend, ignoring the footpath that bears right and descends more steeply to the Monsal Viaduct.

6. Leave the track before it passes under a bridge, bearing right to join the Monsal Trail at the former station at Upperdale. Turn right and follow it to and across the Monsal Viaduct, then turn left just before the tunnel and take the steep path up to Monsal Head for well-deserved refreshments and maybe an ice cream!

A WALK IN TWO HALVES, THE OUTWARD LEG USING A FORMER RAILWAY TRACK, THE MONSAL TRAIL, PASSING THROUGH ONE OF ITS TUNNELS, THE RETURN LEG TAKING TO FOOTPATHS AND QUIET LANES AS IT PASSES THROUGH TWO PEAKLAND VILLAGES.

From Monsal Head, overlooking the spectacular river gorge of Monsal Dale, a descent is made to the Monsal Viaduct, one of the Peak District's most famous landmarks. This, the tunnels and the tortuous but scenic route through the limestone gorge by the Midland Railway were constructed to link Manchester and London, an impressive feat of Victorian engineering. Not everyone saw the railway as an asset to the dale, however. John Ruskin, artist, poet and conservationist of the time remarked: 'The Valley is gone – and now every fool in Buxton can be in Bakewell in half an hour and every fool at Bakewell in Buxton.'

Our walk follows the route of the trackbed, now a cycle and walkway known as the Monsal Trail, through the 400-metre Headstone Tunnel, then presses on to the former Great Longstone Station. The ornate station building was designed to match the nearby Thornbridge Hall, built in 1859 in the Jacobean style. Nowadays, it is the home of Thornbridge Brewery, the wonderful hoppy smells giving away its proximity to the Trail.

Great Longstone is a thriving village with a school, two pubs, a village green and the fine 13th-century church of St Giles, which has a medieval cross in its churchyard. The main reason for the village's growth was lead mining and shoe making in the 18th century. St Crispin is the patron saint of shoemakers, hence the name of one of the pubs with its sign showing a cobbler at work.

A mile further along the walk is Little Longstone. Much smaller than its bigger sister, the village boasts a fine 17th-century manor house, a quaint old inn, the Packhorse, lovely cottages adorned with flowers in spring and summer, and a delightful little chapel.

THE BASICS

Distance: 4½ miles / 7.2km

Gradients: Fairly steep descent to the Monsal Trail. Any ascent is gradual.

Grade: 2

Approx. time to walk: Allow 3 to 3½ hours

Stiles: Three

Path description: Steps in initial footpath descent, then compacted walkway, field paths and quiet lanes

Maps: OS Explorer OL24, Peak District, White Peak Area

Start point: Viewpoint in front of Monsal Head Hotel. (GR SK 185 715)

Parking: Monsal Head pay-and-display car park, Postcode DE45 1NL

Dog-friendly: On leads where there is livestock and along Monsal Trail if not well controlled

Public toilets: Monsal Head public toilets

Nearest food: Stables Bar and Hobb's Café at Monsal Head

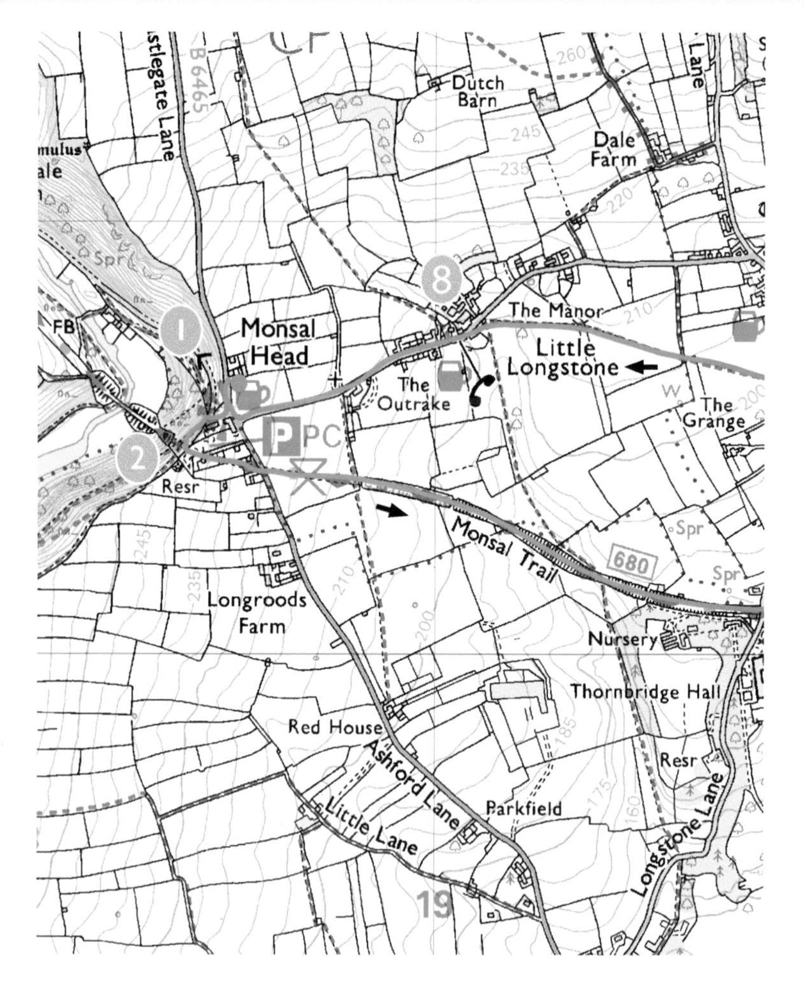

1. Facing the dale at the viewpoint go left, pass in front of Hobb's Café, then take the footpath going down to the right signposted to Monsal Viaduct. Descend steps then turn left as for the viaduct. Follow the narrow path down to the Monsal Trail. Before continuing through the Headstone Tunnel, take time to absorb the stunning valley scenery from the viaduct.

2. Now head back along the Trail into the Headstone Tunnel, re-emerging after 400 metres or so. Keep straight ahead along the Monsal Trail, soon passing through the former Great Longstone and Ashford railway station, which closed in 1962 and is now a private residence. Continue along the Trail. After passing over the second bridge a point is reached where fingerposts to left and right indicate a

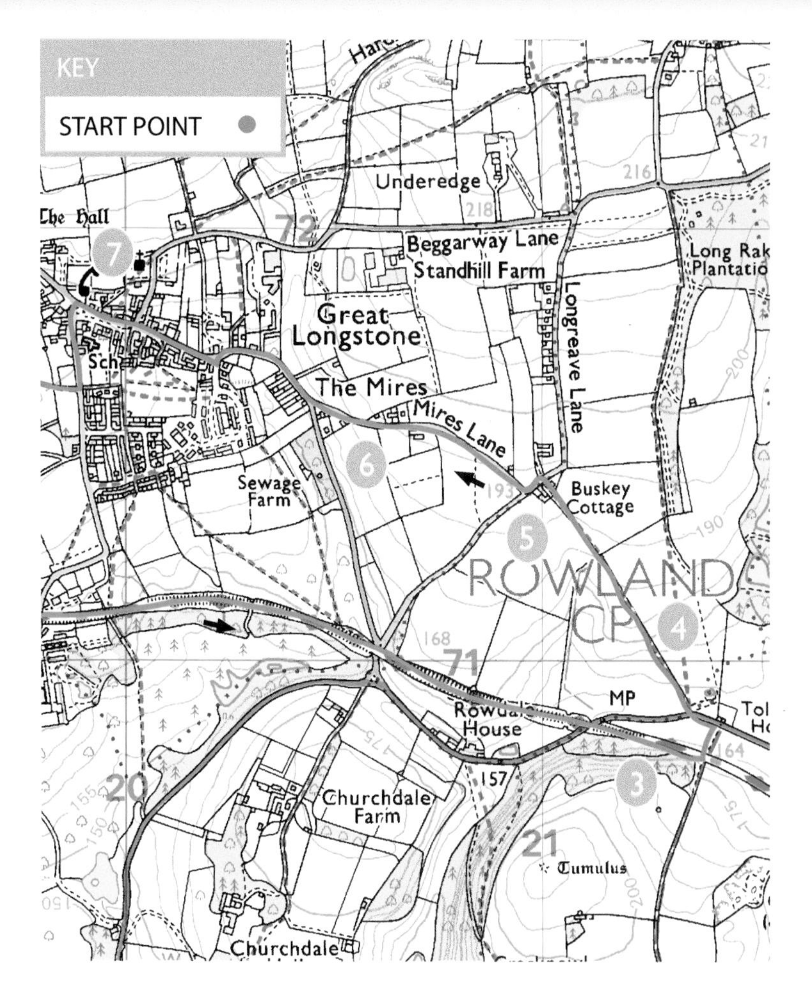

bridleway that is crossed by the Trail.

3. Turn left, go through a gate, and walk across a field to a gate and main road, on the opposite side of which is Toll Bar House. Go left for 100 metres, then cross the road with care and the stile opposite. Two footpaths head off up the large field ahead.

4. Take the less obvious footpath, shown as taking a line bearing slightly left up the field. As the slope begins to level out two gates appear in the wall ahead. Aim for the right-hand gate and cross the adjacent stile. Keep straight on with a wall on your left to the farm buildings ahead. Continue across a stile on the left of a gate then through a squeeze stile to a minor road.

5. Turn left, then right along Mires Lane. Follow the lane to a junction.

6. Turn right into Great Longstone. Walk through the village, passing the White Lion pub, as far as the first road on the left, signposted to Thornbridge Hall. Note the medieval market cross and The Crispin pub sign just ahead at this point.

7. Turn left and continue to a fingerpost and footpath on the right in 200metres. Follow the obvious footpath across fields with stiles, crossing a track en route, to emerge at the road in Little Longstone via a gate. Almost opposite is The Manor mentioned above.

8. Cross the road and continue along the pavement past the Packhorse Inn, cottages and the tiny Victorian chapel to return to Monsal Head.

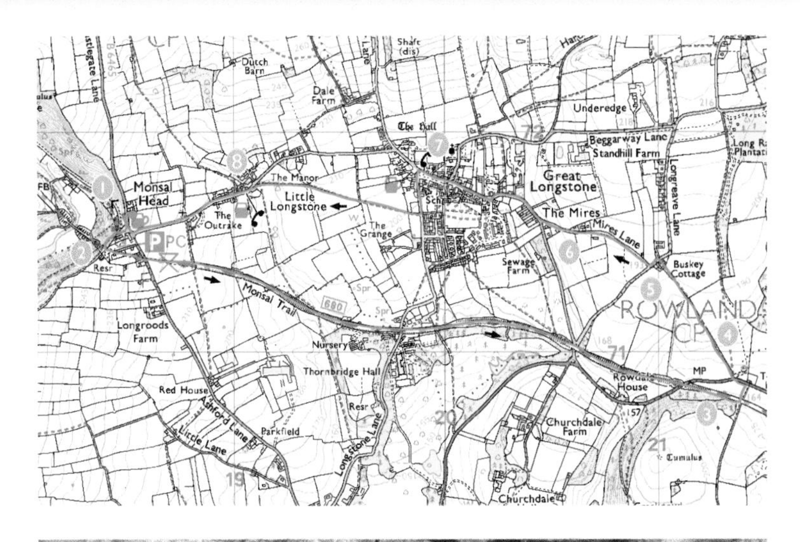
Shaft (dis)
Dutch Barn
Dale Farm
The Hall
Underedge
Beggarway Lane
Standhill Farm
Monsal Head
The Manor
Little Longstone
The Outrake
The Grange
Great Longstone
The Mires
Mires Lane
Longreave Lane
Sewage Farm
Buskey Cottage
ROWLAND CP
Resr
Monsal Trail
Longroods Farm
Nursery
Thornbridge Hall
Rowdale House
MP
Red House
Ashford Lane
Little Lane
Parkfield
Longstone Lane
Churchdale Farm
Tumulus
Churchdale

LITTON

THIS VARIED WALK TAKES IN AN ANCIENT VILLAGE ON THE LIMESTONE PLATEAU, AN 18TH CENTURY MILL HAMLET IN A RIVER GORGE, AND A DELIGHTFUL LIMESTONE DALE, USING A COMBINATION OF QUIET LANES, OLD TRACKS AND FOOTPATHS.

Litton is a picturesque village of stone cottages and lies on the limestone plateau in a sheltered position beneath the escarpment of Litton Edge. Originally a village of lead-miners' cottages and a few small farms, there are also some fine larger houses. At its centre is a village green with a market cross, the base of which probably dates from the 13th century. The stocks are a more recent addition! En route out of Litton one cannot fail to notice the network of narrow fields that were established in early medieval times, when narrow 'strips' of land were cultivated by peasant families.

Further on, in Miller's Dale, the walk passes through the hamlet attached to Litton Mill. This was set up in 1782 by two local farmers, although the present building is mostly 19th century in origin. It was powered by water from the River Wye using Richard Arkwright's water frame. The original mill became notorious for its unsavoury employment practices. Its isolated location presented problems in attracting a workforce. As a solution, poor and orphan apprentices were brought in from London and other cities. These were treated with appalling cruelty, and the graves of many are to be found in local churchyards, one of which is passed en route.

Tideswell Dale is one of the most accessible of the limestone dales. The footpath through it is compacted and enables wheelchair users to sample the delights of a Derbyshire Dale with a stream running through, crags and woodland typical of the dales.

THE BASICS

Distance: 4¼ miles / 6.8km

Gradients: Includes a very gradual half-mile climb and a short but fairly steep descent along a track

Grade: 1

Approx. time to walk: Allow 2½ to 3 hours

Stiles: Three that are adjacent to gates that are usually unlocked

Path description: Well-compacted or tarmac footpaths, a grass track and a quiet lane

Maps: OS Explorer OL24, Peak District, White Peak Area

Start point: Tideswell Dale car park and picnic site just off the B6049 between Tideswell and Miller's Dale. (GR SK 154 742)

Parking: As above

Dog-friendly: On leads where there is livestock

Public toilets: Car park

Nearest food: Red Lion pub at Litton en route.

1. Walk back in the direction of the car park entrance but keep on the right. Follow the footpath signposted to Tideswell alongside a line of mature beech trees. Continue through a gate then straight on with a wall and the road on your left. The path ends at another gate at a road junction.

2. Turn right, and right again to follow the tarmac path uphill to Litton. Bear right with the main road using the lane-cum-pavement in front of cottages. Continue past the post office to a road junction on the right. This is signposted to Cressbrook and Monsal Dale.

3. Turn right here and continue along the quiet walled lane. There are extensive views of the area, as well as the spectacle of wall upon wall that form the boundaries of narrow fields dating from the Middle Ages. The lane is joined by another after half a mile. Keep straight on past Litton cemetery, beyond which the road levels out then begins to descend. Stay on the lane, continuing past a small terrace, New Houses. Further on, pass a cottage on a left-hand bend and continue for another 200 metres to a track and signpost for Litton Mill and Miller's Dale just before a cottage on the left.

4. Follow the track as it doubles back downhill below the road, passing through a gate, and continue to descend with superb views of Miller's Dale and the gorge of Water-cum-Jolly. The small chimney poking out of the hillside next to the track has a flue that runs up the steep hillside from the hamlet below. This took the poisonous fumes away from the lead smelting furnace that was in the gorge before the textile mill became established. Pass through another gate and follow the old, grass track as it zigzags downhill steeply. Pass through a third gate and continue downhill to level ground at the hamlet of Litton Mill. The actual mill, now converted to modern luxury apartments, is on the left here.

5. Turn right and walk through the mill hamlet along the minor road with the River Wye on your left. In 300 metres a footpath emerges from Tideswell Dale on the right.

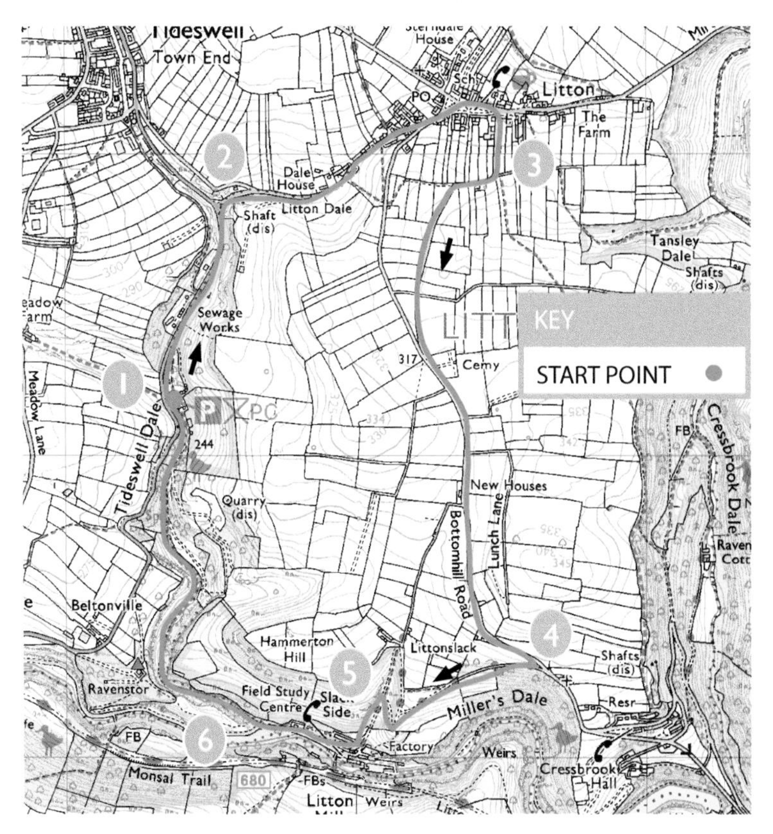

6. Bear right here and continue up the dale, passing old mines in the limestone crags beside the path. Pass through a gate and keep straight on. A little further on, either keep on the left of the stream or cross a footbridge. Both paths lead back to the car park.

BRETTON

THE WALK STARTS AT A HAMLET WITH BREATHTAKING VIEWS OF THE CENTRAL PEAK DISTRICT THEN USES AN ANCIENT TRAIL TO DESCEND INTO A SECLUDED WOODED VALLEY. AFTER WENDING A WAY THROUGH IT, A SHORT, ZIGZAG CLIMB UP A STEEP WOODED SLOPE IS MADE TO REGAIN THE HIGHER GROUND.

In the heyday of lead mining in the 18th and 19th centuries Bretton was a more substantial settlement with a row of miners' cottages between the inn and the location of the Youth Hostel. The Barrel Inn lays claim to being the highest public house in Derbyshire. Undoubtedly, it has the finest views of any Peak District hostelry. The building dates from 1597 but probably did not become a fully fledged inn until the 17th century. To emphasise its historic roots a list of landlords since 1753 hangs on a wall by the bar.

The inn stands alongside what was once the turnpike road from Buxton to Grindleford. The walk starts along Back Lane, an earlier turnpike road replaced by the above from which the panorama ahead is of the hills and moors of the Dark Peak, and Mam Tor is clearly discernible. Further on, the walk takes to a former packhorse trail that linked Eyam with Bradwell, dropping to cross the brook in Bretton Clough at a fording point known as

Stoke Ford. Along the descent there are stunning views up and down the length of Bretton Clough. The word 'clough' means valley with a stream, and there are a number of these in this part of the Dark Peak.

Bretton Clough is very secluded, and in 1745 the farmers of Eyam drove their cattle into the valley to hide them from Bonnie Prince Charlie and his Highlanders on their way south. At this time there were several homesteads in the valley. The ruins of some of these are passed as one crosses the little walled fields.

THE BASICS

Distance: 3½ miles / 5.6km

Gradients: A fairly steep descent for the last 150 metres to the valley bottom and one short, steep climb out of the valley

Grade: 3

Approx. time to walk: Allow 2½ to 3 hours

Stiles: Five

Path description: A mixture of tracks and footpaths in undulating terrain, with a short muddy section in most weathers

Maps: OS Explorer Map OL24, The Peak District, White Peak area

Start point: Bretton, located on a high country road accessible from Grindleford, Eyam or Foolow. (GR SK 201 779)

Parking: On roadside on the uphill side of the Barrel Inn. Postcode S32 5QD

Dog-friendly: Dogs on leads where there is livestock.

Public toilets: Nearest public toilets are in Eyam

Nearest food: Barrel Inn at Bretton

1. Facing the front of the inn take the tarmac lane that runs alongside the left of the building. Follow this down to a couple of cottages that constitute modern-day Nether Bretton, enjoying the expansive views across to Abney Moor and distant Mam Tor. Stay on the lane, which becomes a rough track after The Croft, and follow it up as far as a wooden ladder stile on the left of a gate, with a footpath sign to Stoke Ford.

2. Cross this stile and follow the pleasant track with a wood on your right initially. The track soon enters open ground. Follow it as far as the right-hand bend where the track heads up to farm buildings but keep straight on along an old grassy track, the original packhorse trail that linked Eyam with Bradwell. Continue along this, crossing two stiles situated alongside gates. Keeping a wall on the left with the heather moorland of Sir William Hill to the right, descend to a stile on the left of a gate.

3. Cross this and continue descending the hillside, taking in the stunning views of Bretton Clough en route. The packhorse trail eventually degenerates into a narrow footpath as it winds its way down more steeply into Bretton Clough through birch and oak woodland. At the end of the descent the path meets another that runs through Bretton Clough above a brook. To visit Stoke Ford turn right and follow the footpath in descent for 50 metres or so, then retrace your steps.

4. Turn left, or go straight on if returning from Stoke Ford. Follow the narrow footpath upstream above the brook through wild woodland dominated by silver birch, rowan and twisted, gnarled oak trees. The path passes through two gates, makes a short, steep climb, then passes through more open terrain before bending left into a narrow valley.

5 Cross a stile, pass through a gate and bear left to climb the steep slope by the

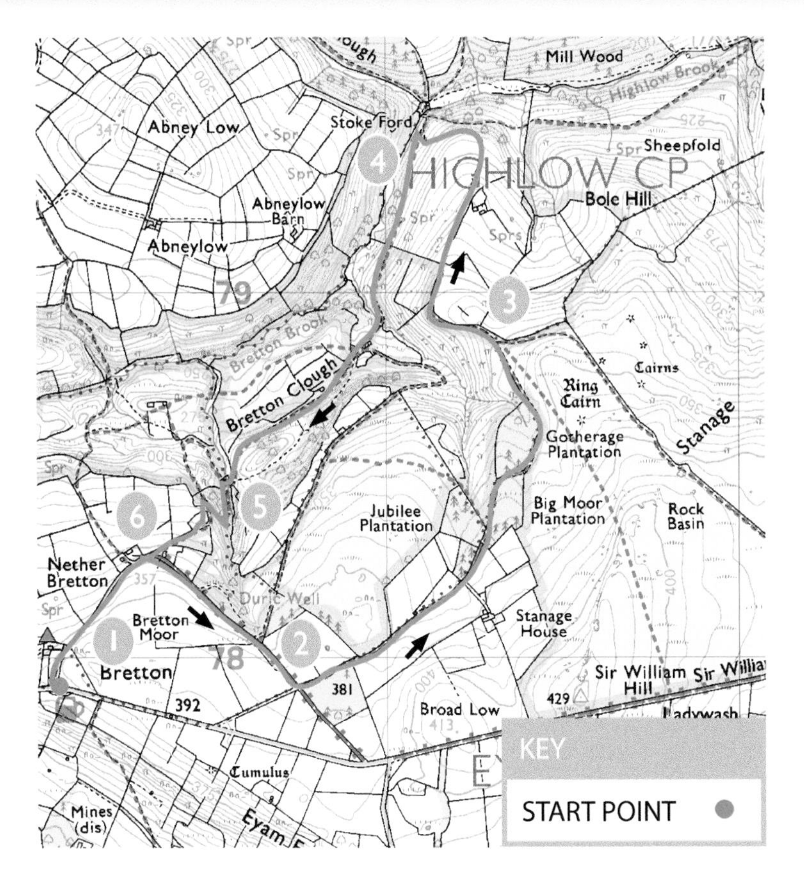

zigzag path. Cross a stile by a gate at the top of the steep slope and follow the still ascending footpath, passing through another gate, before arriving at the tarmac lane used at the start of the walk.

6. Turn right and continue up the tarmac lane back to the inn.

THIS IS A DELIGHTFUL AND VARIED WALK WITHIN A NATIONAL TRUST ESTATE CRISS-CROSSED BY ANCIENT TRACKWAYS. IT PASSES THROUGH A LANDSCAPE THAT IS PART WOODLAND, WILD PASTURE AND HEATHER MOORLAND. ALTHOUGH FOOTPATHS ARE FOLLOWED THROUGHOUT, A ROAD HAS TO BE CROSSED TWICE.

Longshaw was originally part of the Duke of Rutland's shooting estate, Longshaw Lodge being the accommodation. It is famous for its annual sheepdog trials, which are reckoned to be the oldest continuous sheepdog trials in the country. Nowadays, visitors flock to the estate to walk, to explore the rich wildlife and ancient woodlands, or just enjoy refreshment at the splendid visitor centre.

The first part of the walk follows a grassy track with magnificent views of the estate's woodland, wild meadows and heather moorland, as well as the more distant hills and high moors. Entering woodland, bordering the footpath are several very large mounds that are the nests of the hairy wood ant.

Further on, and just off the route, is a Companion Stone – a companion, that is, to a nearby Guide Stoop. Stoops were set up 300 years ago to help travellers find their way to market towns across treacherous moorlands. Longshaw was on an important trading route for salt, silk, wool and lead and is criss-crossed with ancient packhorse trails. Companion Stones are located next to or near Guide Stoops, each bearing an inscription 'pointing towards the future', and are the result of collaboration between local poets, sculptors and masons.

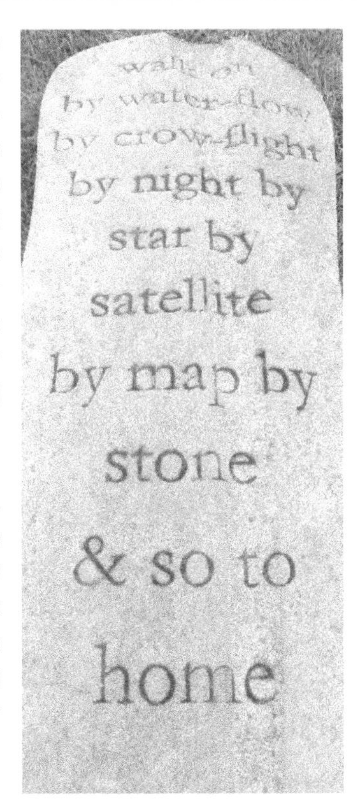

Granby Discovery Barn is passed en route. This is a tiny visitor information centre where you can discover the history and natural history of Longshaw. A little further on, another short diversion is recommended to visit the ancient oak woodland of Padley Gorge, where gnarled and twisted moss-covered oaks provide a habitat for the pied flycatcher and many other bird species.

THE BASICS

Distance: 3 miles / 4.8km or 2½ miles (4km)

Gradients: A few stone steps in descent if the longer walk is selected.

Grade: 1

Approx. time to walk: Allow 1½ hours to 2 hours

Stiles: None

Path description: Straightforward footpaths and old grassy tracks

Start point: Longshaw Estate, Woodcroft pay-and-display car park. Entrance off A6187 about 250 metres south of the Fox House Inn. Grid reference SK 266 800.

Maps: OS Explorers OL 1, Dark Peak Area, and OL 24, White Peak Area

Parking: As above Postcode S11 7TS

Dog-friendly: On leads where there is livestock

Public toilets: Longshaw Visitor Centre / Teashop

Nearest food: Longshaw Teashop. Fox House Inn

1. Head downhill along the footpath to the Visitor Centre. On reaching a signpost, turn left for Wooden Pole Car Park. This climbs a little and comes to a gate. Continue straight ahead, now along a grassy track with exceptional views of the hills and moors of this part of the Peak District.

2. Where the track forks, take the right branch. Bear right soon along the path that leads into Wooden Pole Car Park. Continue through the car park and past the Information Point, then branch right along a footpath just right of a wall. Follow this on the level, then as it descends, through mixed woodland. Continue downhill, where you pass several large wood ant nests on both sides of the path. Carry on until you arrive at a track junction. If you wish to make a detour to visit the Companion Stone, follow the track to the right towards the Visitor Centre for 250 metres. The Companion Stone is just left of prominent old gateposts. It points towards the old Guide Stoop mentioned in the narrative. Retrace your steps to the junction.

3. Continue downhill, signposted Yarncliffe, along a grassy track, now in the open with a fine view of the moor and the lump of rock known as Mother Cap on the horizon. The grassy track joins another at a T-junction.

4. Bear right across a culvert and keep straight on along the broad grassy track, with pines, larch and oak trees to either side. Ignore any other paths. Pass through a gate and continue to a path junction. (For the shorter walk, turn right and follow the path past a pond and through several gates to Longshaw Lodge, the Visitor Centre, and Woodcroft Car Park.)

5. Turn left and continue down to Granby Discovery Barn, which as well as being a shelter contains information about the history and natural history of Longshaw. Continue down to the road. Cross the road with care and go through the gate opposite. Descend steps.

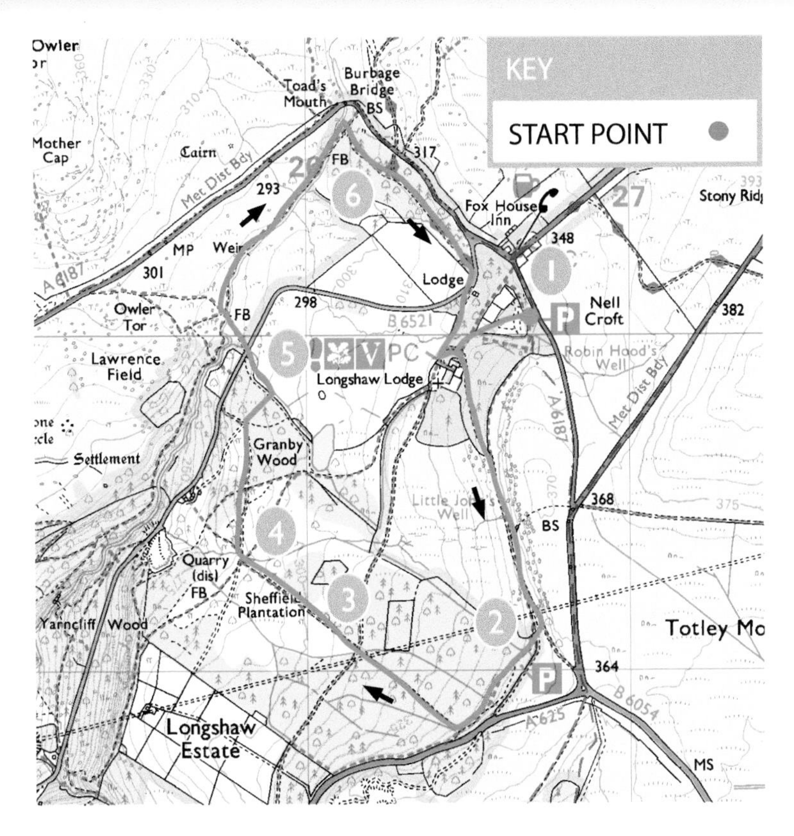

To visit the ancient oak wood of Padley Gorge take the left branch in the path, cross the brook at an arched footbridge, and follow the path down into the wood for a short distance. Retrace your steps to open ground then keep straight ahead with the stream on your right. The main route takes the right branch and crosses Burbage Brook by another footbridge. Continue upstream alongside the brook . In about half a mile re-cross it at a footbridge and follow the stone paved path as it curves upwards into woodland.

6. At a footpath junction bear right across a small stream. Continue through a gate and keep straight on. Pass through a small gate on the left of a large white gate, cross the road with care, then bear right to follow the tarmac lane to the Visitor Centre. There is a Companion Stone and Guide Stoop on the right at the start of the lane. Immediately before the Visitor Centre turn left, then left again for Woodcroft Car Park.

A bridge over Burbage Brook

The Moorland Discovery Centre

THIS WALK CLIMBS IN STAGES TO THE TOP OF A BROAD RIDGE FROM WHERE THERE ARE OUTSTANDING VIEWS OF THE HILLS AND GRITSTONE EDGES SURROUNDING LADYBOWER RESERVOIR. AFTER DESCENDING, A FOOTPATH CLINGING TO THE RESERVOIR'S EDGE IS FOLLOWED BACK WITH BOTH OPEN AND WOODED STRETCHES.

The walk starts at the head of Ladybower Reservoir below the impressive stone-faced Derwent Dam with its two towers. The work on Ladybower Dam, located 3 miles further down the Derwent Valley at Yorkshire Bridge, began in 1935 and was completed in 1945. Unlike the two higher dams, Ladybower was given a grass-covered slope so that it blended into the local countryside.

In creating the reservoir two villages had to be sacrificed, Derwent and Ashopton. The former was located about a mile downstream from the Derwent Dam, the latter where the A57 road viaduct stands now. Some of the villagers were re-housed at the purpose-built estate at Yorkshire Bridge just south of Ladybower Dam.

En route, a high-level bridlepath is followed that passes Lockerbrook Farm. This is owned by The Woodcraft Folk, an international movement for children and young people that believes in equality and cooperation. The former farm is now an outdoor centre offering adventurous activities such as climbing and abseiling, hill walking, weaselling and stream scrambling.

At the highest point on the walk the footpath passes through upland pastures that once belonged to Welbeck Abbey. At the close of the 12th century, the land that now separates the two arms of Ladybower Reservoir was given to the Abbot of Welbeck by King John. Continuous livestock farming here over the centuries has transformed what was once rough moorland into the green grassland that covers the area today.

THE BASICS

Distance: 6 miles / 9.5km

Gradients: A stiff pull at the start of the walk

Grade: 4

Approx. time to walk: Allow 4 to 4½ hours

Stiles: None

Path description: A combination of tracks, footpaths and field paths

Map: OS Explorer OL 1, Peak District, Dark Peak Area

Start point: Fairholmes Visitor Centre, Upper Derwent Valley. (GR SK 173 894)

Parking: As above Postcode S33 0AQ

Dog-friendly: On leads where there is livestock and in open moorland

Public toilets: Fairholmes Visitor Centre

Nearest food: Refreshments at Visitor Centre kiosk. Otherwise Ladybower Inn on A57, and Yorkshire Bridge Inn at Yorkshire Bridge near Ladybower Dam

1. Pass the front of the Visitor Centre, follow the path between the bird feeding areas, and then bear left. Join the road, bear right, and continue as far as the bridge ahead. Turn left here to take the footpath signposted to Derwent Dam West Tower. Bear right at the road, continue alongside the reservoir, then pass through the gate beside the cattle grid.

2. Cross the road to join the forest track signposted to Lockerbrook. Follow this up to the left, through a gate, and past a viewpoint overlooking the dam. When the reservoir is full the cascade pouring over the dam is quite a spectacle. Ignoring any other possibilities, keep straight on up the track. After a right-hand hairpin continue for a further 100 metres to a waymarker with green and black arrows pointing left off the track.

3. Follow this forest path, also signposted to Lockerbrook, to the top of the forest. Go through a gate, then continue up through a field and through another gate.

4. Turn left and follow the stony track to Lockerbrook Farm Outdoor Centre. Continue past, still on the track, to arrive at the brow of a hill with a superb view ahead of Kinder Scout. The track forks at this point.

5. Take the left fork then immediately take the footpath to the left. This turns a left-hand corner. Cross a wooden stile or go through the nearby gate. With splendid views unfolding to the west of Kinder Scout's steep flanks and deeply cut valleys, keep straight on alongside the fenced woodland. In half a mile pass through two gates, where a track comes up from the left, and keep straight ahead as before. When the fence bends left, keep straight ahead following a line of posts. Pass through a gate and continue over a rounded summit from which there is a full 360-degree panorama. Descend and pass through two gates.

6. After the second gate bear slightly left for Crook Hill Farm and Derwent. Contour the hillside, keeping left of the twin peaks of Crook Hill, using the line of waymarker posts as guide. On approaching Crook Hill Farm a sign on the right indicates an 'Alternative Route' through the gate on your left.

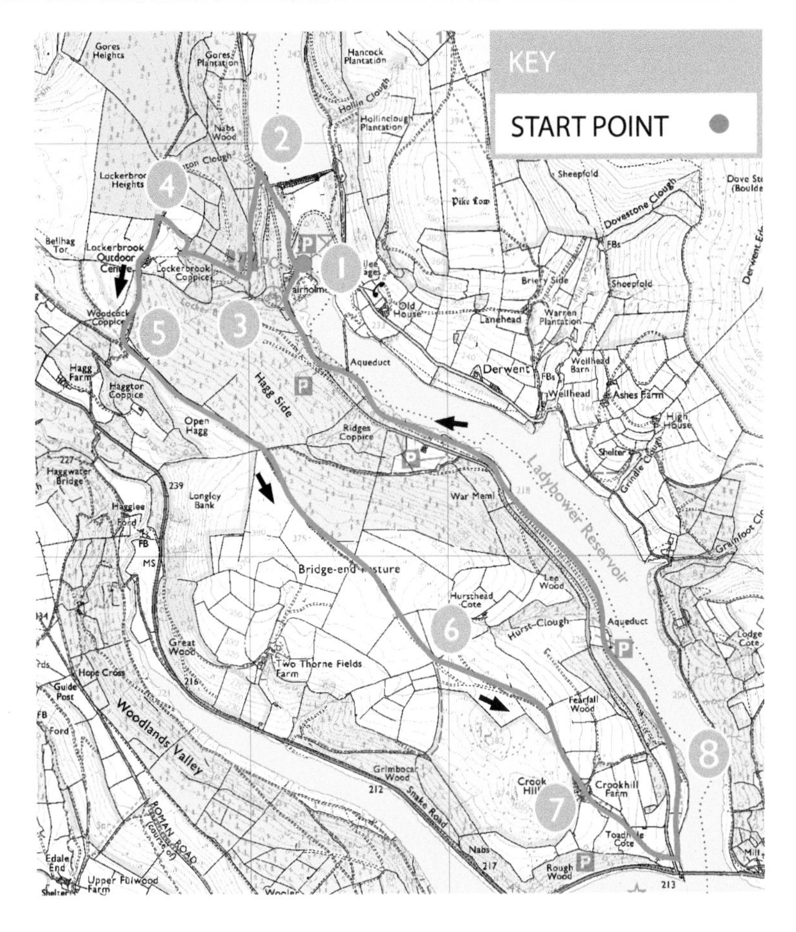

7. Pass through this and bear right down through the field. Go through a gate, cross the farm track and go through another gate on the left of farm buildings. Follow the waymarked path down through fields with gates. The view of Ladybower Reservoir sitting beneath Win Hill to the right and Bamford Edge up to the left is stunning along this section. The field path finally bears left as it descends more steeply by a wood to emerge at the Derwent Valley road.

8. Cross the road, turn right and walk to a gate on the left. Pass through this and follow the Concession Footpath alongside Ladybower Reservoir. The path makes a short descent and ascent via steps to cross a water pipe and, eventually, emerges at Overlook Car Park. Bear right and walk along the pavement, taking the second path on the right to return to the Visitor Centre.

Ladybower and Bamford Edge

Howden Dam featuring one of the famous towers

DERWENT RESERVOIR

A WALK AMONGST THE STUNNING HILL AND VALLEY SCENERY OF THE UPPER DERWENT VALLEY, USING A COMBINATION OF TRACKS AND FOOTPATHS TO PASS OVER HIGH GROUND OVERLOOKING THE RESERVOIRS. IT ALSO INCLUDES A WALK ALONGSIDE DERWENT RESERVOIR AND A DESCENT BY STEPS NEXT TO ONE OF THE DAM'S IMPRESSIVE STONE TOWERS.

Leaving the Visitor Centre at Fairholmes, the lane is followed that curves below the striking Derwent Dam, with its two turreted towers and a central section that becomes a massive cascade when the reservoir is full. The Derwent Dam was completed in 1916. Higher up the Derwent Valley is Howden Reservoir, whose dam has the same design and was completed in 1912. The work on the dams was done by a team of navvies who, along with their families, were housed in the temporary village of Birchinlee, known as Tin Town, the site of which is located on the west side of the Derwent Reservoir.

The two reservoirs with their dams were used during World War II for practice at low-level flying for bombers preparing for the raid on the Ruhr Dams in Germany. The western tower of the Derwent Dam houses a small exhibition describing the epic raid. The feature film The Dam Busters also used the Derwent Valley and reservoirs for some of the flight sequences.

About a mile from the start of the walk, and just beyond the point that our route leaves Ladybower Reservoir and heads for the hills, is the site of the drowned village of Derwent. An information point adjacent to the site provides a picture of life as it was in the village.

Close by the high point on the walk is Pike Low, the site of a Bronze Age burial mound or 'barrow'. Unfortunately, there is no path up the 300 metres of heather moor leading to it, although those who can navigate with map and compass are free to walk to Pike Low, since this is all open access country.

THE BASICS

Distance: 5½ miles / 8.9km

Gradients: A fairly steep half-mile climb, and a shorter but steeper descent

Grade: 4

Approx. time to walk: Allow 4 to 4½ hours

Stiles: Four, of which three have lifting top bars

Path description: Tarmac, then moorland paths and tracks

Map: OS Explorer OL 1, Peak District, Dark Peak Area

Start point: Fairholmes Visitor Centre and car park in the Upper Derwent Valley. (GR SK 173 894)

Parking: Fairholmes Visitor Centre, Postcode S33 0AQ

Dog-friendly: On leads where there is livestock and in open moorland

Public toilets: Fairholmes Visitor Centre

Nearest food: Refreshments at Visitor Centre kiosk. Otherwise Ladybower Inn on A57, and Yorkshire Bridge Inn at Yorkshire Bridge near Ladybower Dam

1. With your back to the kiosk go left past the bird feeding area following the sign to the Dams. Turn right on meeting the road and follow this as it curves right below the impressive Derwent Dam and climbs to Jubilee Cottages. Continue above Ladybower Reservoir along the lane for a further three-quarters of a mile to a footpath sign, gate and stile on the left immediately before the lane descends steeply.

2. Cross the stile, follow the track towards Wellhead Barn, then bear left up the obvious path. Continue up steeply via gates and a stile, not forgetting to look back at the superb view of Ladybower framed by Bamford Edge and Win Hill. After passing through the gate adjacent to a farm building keep straight on up the track as signposted to Derwent Moors. The track bends left through a gate and continues up to another gate with a stile.

3. Cross the stile and follow the track up to the left. After another 150 metres of ascent the track turns right and the going gets easier as it levels out. To the left of the track about 300 metres up a heather slope but out of sight is the ancient burial mound on Pike Low. Continue along the track and bear left as waymarked. Eventually a crossroads of tracks is reached.

4. Keep straight on as signposted to Abbey / Howden Dam. Where the track bends sharp right at a fence, keep straight ahead across a wooden stile. The footpath gradually descends and arrives at a path crossroads with a sign embedded in a cairn. Derwent Reservoir is directly below, and the Derwent Dam is visible from here.

5. Keep straight on as for Howden Reservoir, taking the higher footpath at a fork just beyond the signpost. The path divides again in 200 metres. Bear left down the slope to a wall. Bear right and follow the path beside the wall, staying with it as it descends to the left to a signpost. There is a breathtaking view from here of Howden Dam and Reservoir in its wild moorland setting.

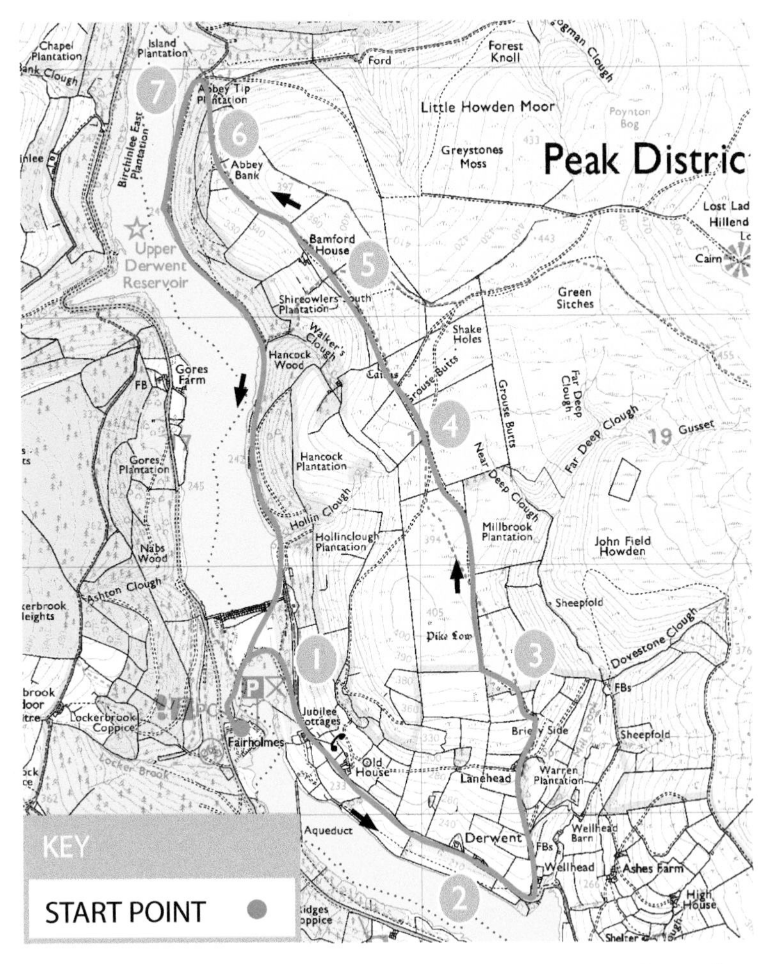

6. Follow the path down steeply to the right, signposted to Abney Grange. Pass through a gate and continue down through the wood to the track that runs alongside Derwent Reservoir.

7. Turn left. Walk along the track for about a mile and a half, then bear right through a gate by the dam. Turn right just beyond the dam wall to descend steps to the foot of the dam. When the dam is overflowing this provides a stunning view of the giant cascade. Continue across the sward to the road, then bear right and retrace your steps to the Visitor Centre.

A STEADY CLIMB ALONG AN OLD BRIDLEWAY LEADS TO A SUPERB VIEWPOINT OVERLOOKING KINDER RESERVOIR AND THE CRAGGY BASIN FORMING THE WESTERN FLANKS OF KINDER SCOUT. A DESCENT TO THE RESERVOIR AND A RIVERSIDE FOOTPATH COMPLETE A FINE EXCURSION.

The village of Hayfield as it appears today is very much a product of the Industrial Revolution. In its heyday several cotton mills provided work for the villagers, in spinning, weaving and calico printing. However, Hayfield's three-storied terraced houses testify to the existence of an earlier cottage industry based on woollen manufacture.

The village has four pubs, two of which, the Packhorse and the George Hotel, are said to date from the 16th century. The inns would have provided accommodation and sustenance to the 'jaggers' and their teams of twenty to thirty packhorses who assembled in the village before heading east across the high, desolate moors.

Hayfield has several other interesting buildings worth a second look. Fox Hall and the adjacent barn on Kinder Road date from 1625. Also on Kinder Road is the former home of Arthur Lowe, the actor most famed for his role as Captain Mainwaring in the TV show Dad's Army. A blue plaque hangs on the front of the cottage where he was born and brought up.

In the 1920s the railway link between Manchester and Hayfield brought 5,000 people every weekend to enjoy the countryside around Kinder Scout. It was from Hayfield that a mass trespass on the grouse moors of Kinder Scout took place in 1932 to highlight the fact that walkers in England and Wales were denied access to areas of open country. Folk singer Ewan McColl celebrated the event in his song 'The Manchester Rambler'.

THE BASICS

Distance: 3¾ miles / 5.9km

Gradients: Prolonged climb over first mile

Grade: 4

Approx. time to walk: Allow 3 to 3½ hours

Stiles: None

Path description: Stony track near the start, then straightforward hill paths

Map: OS Explorer Map OL1, The Peak District, Dark Peak Area

Start point: Sett Valley Trail car park, Hayfield. (GR SK 036 869)

Parking: Sett Valley Trail car park, Postcode SK22 2ES

Dog-friendly: Dogs on a lead where there is livestock

Public toilets: At the car park

Nearest food: Rosie's Coffee and Tea Room on Kinder Road and a choice of four pubs in Hayfield

1. Facing the Countryside Centre, go right, cross the main road at the pedestrian crossing, and keep straight on beside the church to the road running through the village. Turn left, cross the bridge, then head up Bank Street. Bear right and continue up Kinder Road for 400 metres to the Snake Path bridleway on the left, having walked past Rosie's Tea Room and the terraced house where Arthur Lowe lived as a child.

2. Turn left and follow the bridleway up steeply, passing through several gates of one type or another. Stay on the well-worn path, with fine views left across the valley to Lantern Pike. The angle of the slope gradually eases, and the bridleway levels out and passes through a gate, where you enter National Trust land. Now the path bears right and climbs gradually towards a prominent white hut, the Shooting Cabin. Continue to a path crossroads.

3. Turn right to follow the footpath signposted to Snake Inn and Edale. In a short distance at a fingerpost follow the bridleway, which is the right fork. Stay on this as it descends the hillside, ignoring any other possibilities. The view of the craggy western flanks of Kinder Scout cradling the reservoir is quite stunning from this point. Pass through a bridlegate and continue down to join the footpath that runs above the reservoir.

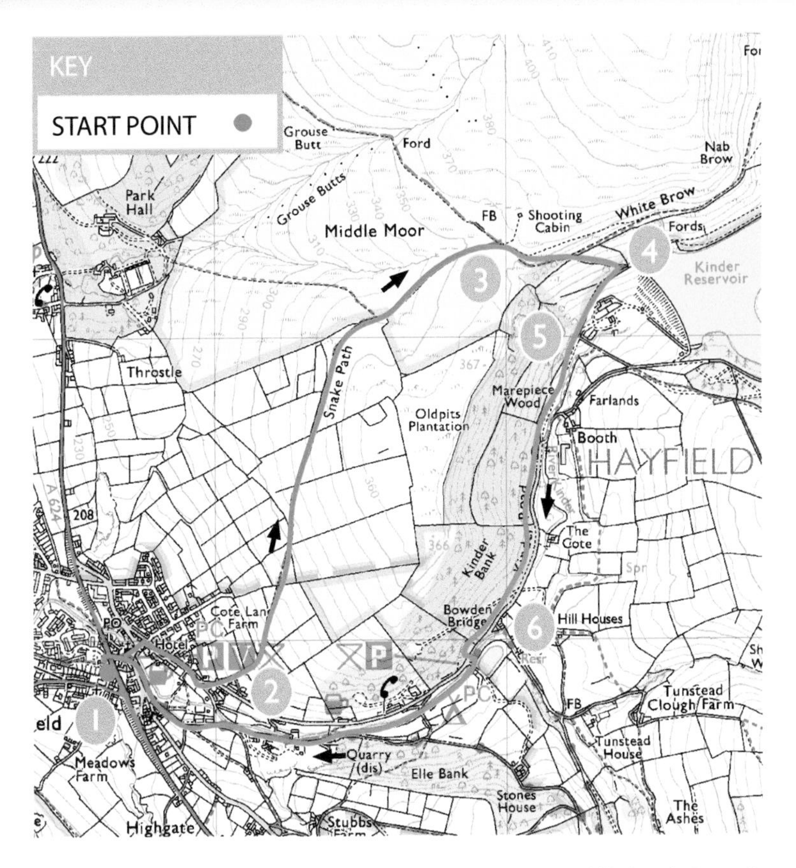

4. Turn right and follow the bridleway downhill. This becomes cobbled as it descends more steeply to merge with a tarmac road.

5. Either keep straight on along the road as far as Bowden Bridge car park. Or, more interesting, turn left, follow the bridleway across the footbridge, then turn right immediately to walk with the infant River Kinder on your right. The footpath joins a minor road which is followed across the river and as far as Bowden Bridge car park.

6. Turn left opposite the car park, cross the bridge, then bear right along the campsite access road. Keep next to the river to follow the riverside path, then a road, back into the centre of Hayfield village. Bear right down the main street and turn left immediately before the church to retrace your steps back to the car park.

GOYT VALLEY

THIS SHORT BUT VARIED WALK IN THE POPULAR GOYT VALLEY STARTS WITH A BRIEF BUT STEEP CLIMB TO TAKE IN THE STRIKING MOORLAND AND RESERVOIR SCENERY THEN DESCENDS THROUGH DELIGHTFUL OAK AND PINE WOODLAND TO EXPLORE THE ROMANTIC RUINS OF ERRWOOD HALL

The Goyt is a deep river valley amidst the moorland west of Buxton. The word 'goyt' derives from the Old English gota, meaning a stream or river. Like the Upper Derwent Valley in the east of the Peak District, the upper valley of the River Goyt was dammed to form the two reservoirs of Fernilee and Errwood.

The Goyt Valley has been a popular tourist destination since Victorian times, when visitors came, much as they do nowadays, to enjoy and walk in this upland valley and on the moors that surround it. Unlike in Victorian times, however, the valley did not have its reservoirs and was home to a working community with farms, a paint works, a gunpowder factory, coal mines, a railway, a school, and the Victorian mansion of Errwood Hall.

The route of the walk climbs a moorland footpath for a view of the Goyt Valley, then descends Shooter's Clough to explore the ruins of Errwood Hall. This was a spectacular mansion built around 1840. It was the lordly home of the Grimshawe family, who had a major influence on the valley in the 19th century, bringing prosperity to the small community.

A mile further up the valley is Goytsclough Quarry. It is reputed to be where the international haulage firm Pickford's started trading in the late 17th century. The means of haulage at that time were trains of packhorses in the charge of packhorsemen, or 'jaggers'. A browse of any map of the Peak District will reveal several references to jaggers, indicating routes that were used to criss-cross the valleys, hills and moors of the Peak linking one market town to another.

THE BASICS

Distance: 2 miles / 3.2km or 1 mile / 1.6km without the hill climb

Gradients: The first half-mile is a steep hill climb

Grade: 3 (or 1 if the easier walk is chosen)

Approx. time to walk: Allow 2 to 2½ hours (or 1 to 1½ hours for the easier walk)

Stiles: None

Path description: Footpaths throughout. A minor stream is crossed on stones which could be a problem in heavy rain.

Maps: OS Explorer OL 24, White Peak Area

Start point: Errwood Car Park in Goyt Valley, situated on the west side, and near the head of, Errwood Reservoir. (GR SK 012 748)

Parking: Errwood Car Park in Goyt Valley

Dog-friendly: On leads in areas of open access

Public toilets: 200 metres east of the Errwood Dam alongside Goyt Lane

Nearest food: Cat and Fiddle Inn on A537, accessible from Errwood car park

1. Facing the reservoir, walk to the right through the car park, and then turn right as signposted for Stake Side. The path climbs steeply. Continue through gateposts and keep straight on uphill as for Stake Side. After half a mile of climbing the path reaches a signpost and gate. The stunning views back provide a good excuse to stop frequently on the climb!

2. Continue through the gate as for Shooter's Clough. The path descends gradually through lovely oak woodland, doubling back to follow the stream's descent of the valley. Further down, the path doubles back to the left, signposted Erwood, crosses a minor stream via stones, then continues downhill with the stream now on your right. The path eventually joins a track.

3. Turn right as for Errwood Car Park. In a short distance another track forks left through prominent gateposts.

4. Bear left here to follow the leafy track. This arrives at steps on the edge of the ruins of Errwood Hall. After exploring the ruins, bear left along the woodland footpath with a stream down in a deep gully to the right. Continue along a wooden walkway that crosses the stream and bear right up steps. Continue along Woodland Walk to where it joins another path.

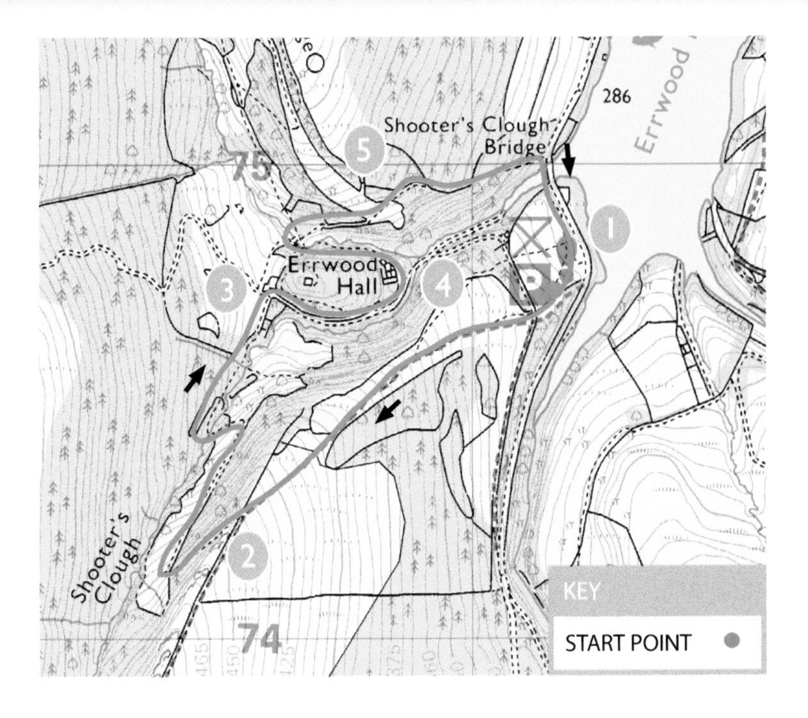

5. Bear right along the continuation of Woodland Walk. This descends through pines and joins the road beside the reservoir. Turn right to finish.

Easier Walk

Head for the information board at the back of the car park. Continue along the footpath for Errwood Hall ruins. After crossing the stream look for steps on the right. Climb the steps, turn right and soon the path bends to the left to the ruins of the hall. Continue as for 4 and 5 above.

WILDBOARCLOUGH

THIS IS A WALK AMIDST UPLAND MOORLAND VALLEYS WITH VARIED AND STUNNING SCENERY. A MIXTURE OF ANCIENT TRACKS AND FOOTPATHS ARE USED FOR ALL BUT THE LAST HALF MILE, WHICH IS ALONG A QUIET COUNTRY ROAD. THE FIRST MILE IS UPHILL.

The walk begins in the beautiful valley of Wildboarclough. It is not certain how the valley obtained its name but it was almost certainly the habitat of wild boar in past centuries. The term 'clough' is a deep valley in these parts. Its softer landscape has more in common with Lakeland valleys, with its scattering of woodland, walled pastures climbing the valley sides, and the mountain-like peak of Shutlingsloe dominating all.

As if to confirm its affinity with the Lake District, the first part of the walk is a climb along an ancient stony track beside Cumberland Brook, as it tumbles down a deep gorge almost hidden by the pines that grow alongside the brook.

The landscape changes abruptly, however, as the track heads up on to desolate moorland, then follows a moorland stream which becomes the infant River Dane at a confluence of streams. This is a remote and beautiful spot with two packhorse bridges, one of which is the splendid 16th-century high-arched Panniers Bridge providing the perfect setting for Panniers Pool below it. The pool acquired its name because the ponies with their heavy panniers would have been allowed to pause here for a drink.

The 'Y'-shaped confluence is known as Three Shires Head, and the three counties of Staffordshire, Derbyshire and Cheshire meet here. It was a place where, in the 19th century, lawbreakers or coiners evaded capture by crossing into a neighbouring county as it was only possible for police to act within their own county boundaries.

THE BASICS

Distance: 4¼ miles / 6.8km

Gradients: Includes a strenuous climb along a stony track for the first mile

Grade: Four

Approx. time to walk: Allow 3 to 3½ hours

Stiles: Three

Path description: A combination of tracks and footpaths with avoidable occasional wet sections. The last half mile is along a quiet road.

Maps: OS Explorer Map OL24, The Peak District, White Peak Area

Start point: Clough House car park, 1km north of Wildboarclough. (GR SJ 987 698)

Parking: Clough House car park. (SK11 0BD)

Dog-friendly: A two-metre descent of steep iron steps could cause problems with some dogs. On leads where there is livestock

Public toilets: None

Nearest food: Crag Inn, Wildboarclough

1. From the car park cross over the brook, passing left of Clough House Farm. At the road go straight across and through the gate to follow the track signposted to the Cat and Fiddle Inn. Continue across a footbridge and uphill along the stony track, soon passing through a gate. The walking is easier up on the right of the track overlooking Cumberland Brook as it descends through the wood-lined gorge. After half a mile the track comes to a gate and stile.

2. Pass through the gate and bear right up the winding track. This climbs for another half mile and levels off just before arriving at a gate and main road.

3. Cross the road with care, step over the metal barrier and descend steep iron steps to enter a field. Continue across a stone stile, then bear slightly left and descend to join an old track. (The retaining wall that the steps descend is about 2 metres high and could pose a problem with dogs. An alternative would be to turn left and walk alongside the main road for 350 metres, then to take the farm track that doubles back down to the right. Keep above the farm and bear right, passing through a gate to re-join the main walk at the old track.)

4. Turn right, follow the old track through a gateway, then turn left immediately. Continue downhill with a wall on the left. On meeting a wall ahead, bear right as waymarked and continue with a wall on the left. Any wet sections can be avoided up on the right of the old track. On reaching a gate, pass through this, cross a bridge over a stream, and keep straight on to Panniers Bridge at Three Shire Heads.

5. After pausing to absorb the beauty of this remote spot in the moors, continue on the same side of the river, the River Dane, along the gradually ascending track. This eventually levels out and comes to a gate where it meets a tarmac lane. Along this section there are some fabulous views south of the Dane Valley and the ridges formed by the gritstone crags of the Roaches area.

6. Bear right, then left just beyond a cottage through a gate with a footpath sign. Follow the path across the moor, negotiating the odd wet patch. Ignore a gate up to the right and, instead, bear left with the main footpath. Cross a wooden stile with a dog gate, then keep straight on (yellow waymark) to emerge at a main road.

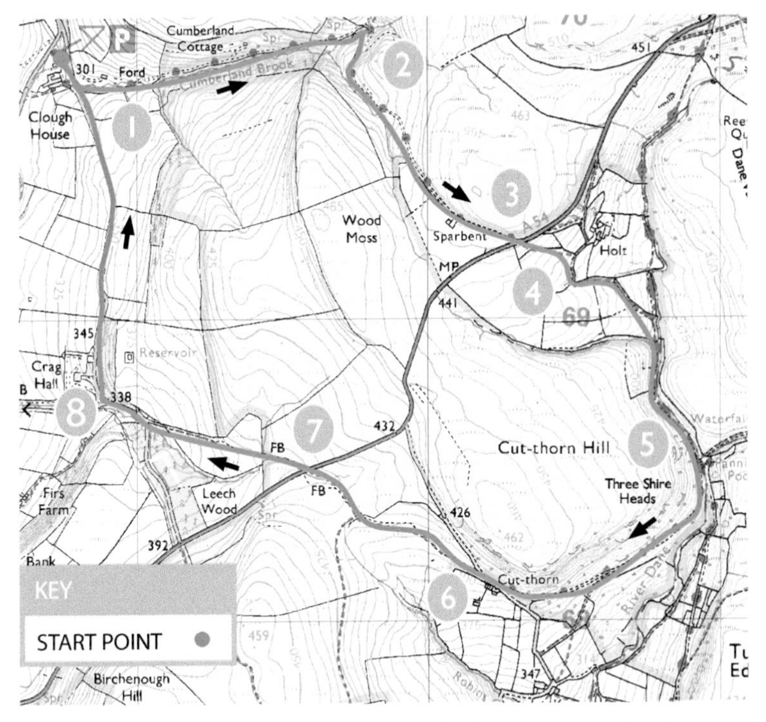

7. Cross the road and the wooden stile opposite. Sections of duckboard ahead keep you out of the bog. Continue through a gate and downhill along the path, with a superb view of Shutlingsloe across the valley. Any wet or boggy parts along the path can be avoided on one side or the other. The path becomes a wet, stony track for a few metres before meeting a road. Continue downhill alongside the road to a junction in 150 metres.

8. Turn right and follow the quiet road back to Clough House.

ABOUT THE AUTHOR

Norman has climbed and walked both in the UK and abroad since his teens. On becoming a father he began to plan walks to suit a young family, which resulted in his first publication in the 1980's, Family Walks in the White Peak. This spawned a nationwide series for Scarthin Books and Norman himself wrote a further five Family Walks guides.

As a teacher for nearly twenty years, he was able to introduce young people to the wonders and potential of the great outdoors. Since leaving the profession and taking up work as manager at Foothills, a Sheffield outdoor equipment specialists, he has led regular guided walks throughout the Peak District. Although now retired, he continues to be in demand as a walking guide.

He is also author of two Peak District Day Walks guidebooks, published by Vertebrate Publishing. As with the Family Walks guides, this is also promising to develop into a series covering major hill walking areas in the UK.

He continues to explore the Peak District with his wife, Sue, and hopes his latest project for Bradwell Books helps others of all ages enjoy its delights.

Special thanks to my wife Sue for recording the walks, providing critical feedback,
and being good company.